NINETY AND NINE

There were ninety and nine that safely lay
In the shelter of the fold;
But one was out on the hills away,
Far off from the gates of gold;
Away on the mountains wild and bare,
Away from the tender shepherd's care.

'Lord, Thou hast here Thy ninety and nine,
Are they not enough for Thee?'
But the shepherd made answer,
'This of mine has wandered away from me.
And although the road be rough and steep,
I go to the desert to find my sheep.'

NINETY and NINE

An Autobiography

Marjorie Ward

Marjorie Ward

ONYX PUBLISHING

Published by
Onyx Publishing
Brendon Books
Bath Place
Taunton
TA1 4ER

Design and typesetting by
EX LIBRIS PRESS

Printed in Great Britain by
Cromwell Press
Trowbridge
Wiltshire

ISBN 0-9532876-1-0

*To Ernest
my husband
and my best friend*

CONTENTS

PART ONE

PART TWO

PART THREE

PHOTOGRAPHS

Front cover: the author in 1943
Back cover: the author with her daughters, 1951
Frontispiece: the author
Between pages 36 and 41:

Between pages 131 and 136:

~ PART ONE ~

NINETY
AND
NINE

1

I was born on the 8th March 1923, at Buckingham Road, Harlesden, London, NW10. We were twins, Winifred and Marjorie Hildyard-Todd, but it cost my mother dear, for shortly after the birth we were all taken to Park Royal Hospital where on the 30th of May my mother died. Neither my sister nor I were given much chance of survival, as we each weighed barely four pounds.

A few weeks after my mother died, we were accepted into John Groom's Orphanage at Clacton-on-Sea, Essex.

We were mainly cared for by Miss Kidman, who I believe was in charge of the Baby's Home. When Winifred was just fourteen months old she died of a weak heart. She was buried at Clacton. Until the age of ten, I grew up thinking that I had no other relatives. I lived at John Groom's until I was fifteen years of age. My experiences there have influenced me throughout the rest of my life.

John Groom, born on the 15th August 1843, was the third child of a large family. His parents, although poor, were honourable Christian people. John's father died when he was only ten and he immediately set about finding work as an errand boy to help his mother bring up her family. He eventually became a Master Silver Turner and Engraver and had his own business which was carried on by his sons.

At the age of sixteen, he became an infant Sunday school teacher and at eighteen years of age he began preaching in the open air and at cottage Bible meetings. He became very popular with all sorts of men, helping the very destitute and lowest of fallen humanity. He visited prisons and police courts, and when asked to pray for known burglars and criminals in their last hours of life, he often went into their slum homes to do so.

At twenty-one years of age, John Groom became a Superintendent of a mission in Harp Alley near Farringdon Market and later he served as a lay pastor to Woodbridge Chapel, Clerkenwell, in southeast London.

Seeing all the poverty and degradation of the masses of people, particularly young children and crippled girls, he felt the need to do something to help. The crippled children, who were deemed a burden to their parents, were sent out at four in the morning to sell artificial flowers at street corners so as to gather coppers to supplement the family income. They could work as long as seventy hours a week. Many died through hunger or tuberculosis brought about by malnutrition and the terrible conditions in which they lived and worked. Something had to be done to help these children, for this was in the days when Charles Dickens was writing, where Oliver Twist, Fagin and other characters were not figures of fun or of the imagination, but caricatures of real people and the social conditions that the masses were living under.

First of all John Groom began providing breakfasts for these children. Eventually he noticed that the artificial flowers were being imported from the continent. It occurred to him that if he could learn the trade of making these flowers to the standard of the imported ones, he could teach the flower girls and women. So in a house in Seckforde Street began the Crippled Girls Industrial Training Branch. John Groom adopted the rose as the emblem for his organisation. The business flourished and many hotels and high establishments bought the artificial flowers. The demand for them grew and grew.

John Groom was still acutely aware of the plight of the orphaned children and in 1888, when three little girls were found homeless in the streets of the city, John took them into his own house where he and his wife cared for them. This experience made him decide to found his own orphanage. After many attempts to find suitable accommodation, a freehold plot of land was purchased in The Old Road at Clacton-on-Sea, Essex and so began the second phase of his work. He really loved this orphanage. The last sounds he heard before he died, during Christmas 1919, were his much-loved children singing Christmas carols outside his home.

Four homes had been built on the west side of the Old Road and later a crescent of six homes was built on the east side. A large meadow ran the whole length of the Crescent homes and joined onto the meadow was a big shelter where the children could play in the dry on a rainy day. Also in the shelter was built a gymnasium where the children practised their dancing and drilling ready for the performances they would be giving on the fête days. The west-side houses were named Snowdrop, Forget-me-not, Buttercup and Daisy. The six Crescent homes were named Bluebell, Wallflower, Lily, Mignonette, Rosebud and Pansy. In 1933 two more houses were built opposite the large fête field. One was called Violet and this was used as the 'tweenies' home, for children aged between five and seven. The other house was named Daffodil and this was our hospital, where a qualified sister nursed the children through their childhood ailments. Before then, Daisy had been used for that purpose.

Each of the Crescent homes had two dormitories, one each side of the staircase, with the housemother's bedroom in-between. This had glass panels so that both dormitories could be observed. At the top of the staircase was the linen cupboard that housed, apart from the bed sheets, the Sunday clothes and shoes. Downstairs, in the centre was the hall, narrower at the back because of the broom cupboard that was partly under the stairs, and wider at the front with a large ornate front door. On one side of the hall was the housemother's sitting room and at the back of that the kitchen, with a big welsh dresser and a black pot-board underneath for the kettles, steamers and saucepans. On the other side of the hall was the dining room that was also used as a playroom. Leading off from the dining room was the scullery and downstairs toilet, which could also be reached from the back yard. From the back yard, the toilet, scullery, kitchen and coalhouse-cum-bucket store could each be reached by its own set of three steps. In the middle of the yard was a small drain that flushed away the water when it rained; although many were the times when it rained so hard it became flooded. We often had to try to brush the water away, particularly in the summer time after a severe thunderstorm.

My first recollection of living at John Groom's is at the age of three or four when I was sitting on the knee of Miss Sheeny, the housemother at Rosebud house, watching the big snowflakes coming down. She was dressed all in black, with a long hobble skirt and was jiggling me up and down. Little Phyllis (Singleton), my friend, just a few months older than me, was standing near when suddenly in the midst of the laughter I remembered that it was bath night. I stopped playing and said to Miss Sheeny, 'Its bath night tonight. Promise you won't smack us in the bath.'

She promised. I felt so relieved and happy, and continued playing. But that night when I stood up to get out of the bath I received the most fearful thrashing. This I can never forget, even seventy-five years on. It is something I have always kept in mind, for however naughty my own children might be I resolved never ever to humiliate them.

However, each year the housemothers had three weeks holiday and we had, as we called them, a 'summer holiday mother.' Well, Miss Sheeny went on her holiday and this particular year we had a lovely holiday mother called Miss Booth. We could not believe that anyone could be so nice with all of us. I remember that her hair was just turning grey and that it was very wavy, and above all that she had lovely kind brown eyes. She had such a lovely face that when she laughed she made us laugh too. Inevitably came bath night. I remember it all so plainly. She had told us stories and laughed and joked with us, but I had yet to stand up and get out of the bath. I remember clinging to the sides of the bath and saying in a troubled voice,

'You won't smack me will you? I have tried to be good.'

'Smack you dear? Of course not, you silly little girl.'

I still insisted.

'Don't smack me will you?'

I remember her turning to the house-girl, Rosie Tiffin, and asking

'Whatever is the matter?'

By this time fear had completely overtaken me and I was sobbing. I remember it all so well as if it were yesterday. She lifted me out of the bath very gently and dried me, chatting all the time. We had three wonderful weeks with Miss Booth and at the end of this time it was with many tears that we said goodbye. In fact, we clung to her and begged her not to go. She told us not to worry. The next hour or so passed and we anticipated the arrival of Miss Sheeny with deep foreboding and fear. When we saw her approaching we became frightened and tearful, but we also saw Miss Booth talking to her and then they went together over to Snowdrop, Matron's house. It was past my bedtime, but no one was bothering. I could feel the excitement in the house and suddenly the bigger girls very excitedly shouted,

'Here she comes!'

And there she was, our lovely Miss Booth. She told us that she was now our housemother for good. We all yelled 'Hooray!' and it was a very happy little girl that went to bed that night.

2

In our house we had an old organ that stood in the corner of the dining room, near the door that led into the scullery. On Sunday afternoons, in my very early days, we had the long tables pushed up against the wall with a long form on top. Some of us sat on the forms while others sat on the tables. Mother would then play hymns on the organ and we would have a little Sunday school. We were so well behaved - too scared to move for fear of falling off the forms! Happily this did not last for long. The old sanatorium, which had been used in the First World War as a soldiers' convalescent hospital, became our Sunday school and was also used for our Sunday evening services. The old organ remained in our house for years, and I was reprimanded one day when Mother went to play the organ and could not get the pedals down. The pedals were very wide and covered with a thick material. Much to her consternation, it was discovered that I had hidden my ball under the pedals. We did not have many balls to play with so I thought that the old organ would be a good place to hide one. I was not allowed to play with a ball for a week, for by hiding one, I was making sure that no one else would have a chance to play with it. We were always told to 'share and share alike' in Rosebud house.

We did not have many personal possessions at John Groom's but throughout each year there was a series of regular treats to look forward to. For example, on our birthdays we always received a birthday card, a hair slide or hair band, a handkerchief and two pence, in a birthday packet.

Each Christmas was a very exciting time and for weeks before, there was great preparation. The dining room was thoroughly cleaned. I well remember having to scrub the painted walls in readiness for the decorations. Mother and the older girls would decide on a theme. My most impressive memory is that of the year we did a summer and winter display. One half of the room had a winter theme with lots of cotton wool attached to strands of cotton and hung from the ceiling as snow. The other half of the room was decorated with flowers made out of crepe paper, which were very realistic. Over the top of the bookcase we had a big piece of red crepe paper with 'A Merry Christmas' written on it with cotton wool. This may ring a bell with my own children, for years later I used the same idea for our chimneybreast.

A couple of nights before Christmas the Salvation Army used to play carols in the road at the back of our houses. I loved to hurry into bed so that I could lay and listen to them. My bed was by the back window. To me this event signified that Christmas was really coming.

On Christmas Eve we put our socks at the foot of the bed, ready for Father Christmas. He came! Each child had a sugar mouse at the toe of her sock, some form of confectionary and a game. For the older girls there was a small useful present such as a diary, perfume or an autograph book.

On Christmas morning the house-girls gave the children breakfast in bed. This was a way to keep us upstairs so that the tables could be prepared for the Christmas dinner. After we had had our breakfast we used to get into bed with each other, read stories or play games until Mother told us we could get dressed. We put on our Sunday best and then looked out of the big front windows, waiting our turn for Father and Mother Christmas to come along, ringing a bell and pulling a big cart.

Father and Mother Christmas were two of our workmen dressed up, and they stopped at each house in turn to deliver the parcels sent to the children at Groom's by their relatives. The parcels were taken into the warm kitchen, put on a big white scrubbed table and then mother would hand them out. I knew that there would not be any for me, for I had no one. I used to go and hide under the table so that nobody would see my disappointment. This disturbed dear Mum (Miss Booth) so she wrote to a friend in Kent called Miss Goodman, who became my 'lady' friend. Miss Goodman wrote letters to me, and I was surprised and delighted when I also began to receive a Christmas parcel from her.

Eventually we all sat down to our Christmas dinner and waited for 'Uncle' (John Groom's son Alfred who had taken over the work of his father), to come and carve the turkey. What a huge one it was! How they managed to do all that they did for us at that time, really surprises me, when one thinks of the terrible Depression in the early 'thirties'. When Uncle came in to see us we would sing a carol to him before the jollification started. It was a splendid meal with Christmas pudding, oranges, apples and crackers. Then after dinner, when all the washing up was done, with extra hands helping, we would go upstairs to rest on our beds ready for the big party which was held in the Holiday Home, the big house adjoining Snowdrop (Matron's house). The Holiday Home was built especially for the use of the girls and women working in the Crippleage at Edgware, to give them a holiday by the seaside. The bedrooms all had separate cubicles.

When we first arrived at the party we were shown into the huge dining room, with all the tables laid out for the different houses (two houses to a table) so there was plenty of happy chatter going on. We had a sumptuous tea and then the tables were cleared and pushed to one side, ready for the games to start. We played all the old familiar ones: Postman's Knock, Blind Man's Buff, Oranges and Lemons, Musical Chairs and so forth. At about eight o'clock Father Christmas again appeared in his sleigh, to hand out a present to each one of us. One year it was Mr Cooke, the Principal. He came in through the window this time, right where I was sitting, knowing full well that my reaction would be a great yell of surprise. He was a wonderful man and I know that we all loved him, for whenever I saw any of the 'Old Girls' at the Reunions they all spoke of him with great affection. At almost midnight we would make our way home (the little ones having gone home earlier), all of us thoroughly tired but happy.

The next day we did not get up until 9 or 10 a.m. It was Boxing Day and once again we were in for a treat. After dinner, at about three o'clock, we all went back to the Holiday Home. Everything had been cleared away and cleaned, and all the chairs had been put into rows. A little platform had been erected and we were entertained by the artists staying at the Ambleside Hotel at Clacton. They did little sketches, and danced and sang for us. At the end of their performance we were each given a whole sixpence! What two glorious days they were. But Christmas was not over yet, for each house then planned its own party and each of the older girls was allowed one friend from another house as her guest. As I look back after all these years I cannot but marvel at the tremendous amount of work that went into giving us such wonderful Christmases.

3

In order to raise funds for the orphanage we had weekly fête days in the summer, from the first Tuesday in June to the first Tuesday in September. From the beginning of October to the first fête day we practised very hard for these events. A Miss Lillian Maloney was our dance teacher and another lady (whose name I have failed to remember) played the piano. We had two different programmes to put on, on alternate weeks. And very good they were too. One week we did our National Dances of England, Ireland, Scotland and Wales. The second week we performed dances from the Commonwealth. Our dressmakers, a Miss Fitt and a Miss Church made all the costumes. Apart from that they made all our school uniforms and summer dresses as well.

I have a special memory of the 1937 fête. We danced a programme depicting 'The Four Corners of the World Under British Rule.' In the middle of the field we had a big white dais on which stood one of the taller girls representing the Statue of Liberty. After completing our dances we would form a tableau around the statue and then would sing Land of Hope and Glory as a grand finale. One week as we started to sing, a man jumped onto the platform and started to conduct the music. Immediately all the visitors (which that day numbered eleven thousand) stood to sing with us. The following week we were asked to repeat that programme. When the finale came, up popped the same man, but this time he had a pianist with him. Their names were Eric and Stanford Robinson, the famous conductor and pianist. Storm clouds of the Second World War were gathering – I cherish that memory to this day.

The previous year had seen the Coronation of the Duke and Duchess of York, who on the abdication of Edward VIII became King and Queen. We did our National programme, entering the arena with two little girls dressed as the King and Queen. Six girls dressed as high stepping horses pulled them along in their carriage. I was one of them. When the King and Queen were safely sitting on their throne we did our dance, with our harnesses jingling and our headdresses of brightly coloured feathers jigging up and down. Years later, I met people who had been to these fête days and who said what a wonderful time they had. They showed me the photographs they had taken at the fête and I was actually in them.

The fête used to start at two o'clock in the afternoon and finish at about half past ten in the evening. During the afternoon Uncle Alfred and a Mr Abbott used to be in charge of the games. First, there was the chariot race. The chariots were just boxes on wheels with handles but they were decorated with artificial flowers. The men would pull them along with their wives or sweethearts in. Then came football on roller skates and children's races. The crowds loved it.

Before each game commenced Uncle Alfred and Mr Abbott would choose their team. They did not have to beg for volunteers, as the members of the audience would rush down the steps to take part. The volunteers were lined up and individuals were picked out. The teams would then link arms and march up and down singing the old war songs such as Pack Up Your Troubles and It's a Long Way To Tipperary, to get them all in a happy mood. We could hear them roaring with laughter in our homes, as we were getting ready for our performances that began at six o'clock and lasted until eight o'clock. Teas, drinks and light refreshments were served throughout the afternoon and evening. In the interval of our performance, Uncle would make a speech and contributions were collected. Quite a substantial sum was raised and he always let people know at the end of the evening how great a sum it was. In his speech one day we learnt that one of our John Groom's girls had become Mayoress of London. Since then we have had other girls that have risen to prominence. One is a titled Lady today. After his speech the fun and games would resume and at nine o'clock came the relay race. There were nine men against six of us orphanage girls. Of course we were given a head start, and when we ran to the person holding the handkerchief we realised he was closer than the man holding the handkerchief for the men's side. We never lost a race. After the race each girl participating was given three pence. Then came the Tug of War (this time six men to twelve of us girls). Mr Abbott and Uncle Alfred would again choose the teams, making sure that they chose the least hefty looking men. Again we were never beaten.

At ten o'clock the older girls took part in the Fire Display. This became the highlight of the evening, both for the visitors and us. Also many of the local people would come just to see it. One schoolteacher came and reckoned that she heard my voice shouting 'Fire!' above everybody else's. We used to put on our nightdresses over the top of our ordinary clothing, and stand in the corridor of the Holiday Home while Mr Nash (the foreman of all the male workers) came to light the fireworks which had been erected on the walls and balcony. When we heard the first bang we would rush onto the balcony yelling 'Fire!' The workmen dressed up as firemen with their fire helmets on, would come running with a ladder. They would rush onto the middle of the balcony to let down the chute. We lay headfirst onto the chute and then a fireman would push us down. Other firemen were waiting at the bottom of the chute to shake it and help us out. Once released we would run back into the building yelling 'Fire!' to have another turn, or to have a go on a fireman's back, or on the 'swing'. This was a webbed seat that was attached to wires. The firemen would turn a handle furiously and we would swing down to the ground. We longed to be old enough to participate in the fire drill. The first time that we could, we would run onto the balcony and just shout 'Fire!' being too scared to do anything else, but gradually the thrill and excitement got the better of us and we loved it. People used to come to the fête just to see the spectacular fire drill at Groom's.

4

In spite of all this jollification, we each had our daily jobs to do. We were awakened at half past six each morning. We had to make our own beds, and by this I mean strip them. I was caught covering mine over quickly one morning and Mother ordered me to strip it all off and do it all over again. I was cross at being found out, but I never tried that one again!

From about the age of nine, we had a job to do before breakfast, which was at half past seven. My first job was to clean all the brasses in the house, which meant all the light switches and doorknobs. I did not mind this too much as you could just get on with the job without waiting for anyone. Other jobs such as dusting the dormitories while someone else swept them, were often slower, as you might have to wait for someone who was slow getting up. After dusting we had to put on the white quilts and make sure that all the beds were straight, and that the line on the quilts was absolutely straight as you looked up the row of beds. Both sides of the quilt had to be tucked in, envelope fashion, as in hospitals. What training! I still make my beds in the same way today. Each dormitory had twelve beds. Two were by the back window with a screen, and the doorway next to them. There were three beds the other side of the door, with a doorway to Mother's bedroom next to them. The other side of the room had six beds between two radiators, and then one bed just outside the bathroom door, or Mother's bathroom door, depending which dormitory you were in.

At eleven years of age we each became responsible for one

of the little ones. We had to look after their clothing and every night when they undressed for bed, we had to go through their clothes to make sure there were no buttons missing or holes in their socks. If there were, we had to mend them for the next day.

By the age of twelve the workload had increased. One job was to clean the downstairs toilet. This was done with 'earth' and nothing else. After this, all the flights of steps into the yard had to be scrubbed. On Saturdays the yard had to be swilled down with soda water and scrubbed with a hard broom. A couple of times, I had to get down on my hands and knees and literally scrub it all over because the soda water and yard broom did not get it clean enough. When there was to be an inspection by Matron or the Councillors I remember having to clean the aluminium buckets to make them shine - a futility now I come to think of it.

The scullery contained a sink, two big wooden draining boards and a large shoe rack, which held twenty-four pairs of shoes. Two girls had to clean all the shoes every night, directly after tea. We were never allowed into the house in our outdoor shoes.

After completing our Saturday jobs we were allowed out to play. We had a gardener called George Hutton, but we always called him Mr Polly. Having at that time not read any of H. G. Wells works, I did not know the reason why, but he seemed to like it. He was a nice man, not very tall and quite slim. The extensive gardens, under his care were beautiful, and what is more, he loved his work. On Saturday mornings I used to go and look for Mr Polly, to watch him work and chat to him. Sometimes he used to work in his potting shed, especially if it was a rainy day. I used to help him to plant the seeds. Not only did he see to the flowers, but also to the vegetables and the greenhouse, and I became very interested in helping with these jobs too. He always called me his 'Little Margy.' Sometimes he would bring a bag of sweets and give me some, and I remember one Saturday he gave me so many that when I went home at dinnertime I could not eat at all. It was rabbit stew and I remember having the plate taken away, and then at teatime having to eat it up cold before being allowed the rest of my tea. We were not allowed to leave anything without asking Mother first. Very often we girls would ask Mother if we could leave a piece of gristle or stump of cabbage, and we did not always get away with it. Funnily enough we never asked to leave any of our puddings. They were really lovely: jam roly poly, plain roly poly (with syrup on), Spotted Dick (a great favourite), jam tart (the pastry was superb), rice, semolina or tapioca. At the weekends we had fruit and custard. On Saturdays we were given an apple or an orange, and a Saturday penny to spend at the sweet shop. On Sundays we were given jam on our bread and a piece of cake.

Mr Cooke, when visiting Clacton, would stay at Mr Bangy's house, which was in the grounds of John Groom's but faced onto Old Road. Mr Bangy was one of the workmen for all the general jobs that needed doing. He also looked after the boilers. The boiler house was situated in the middle of the Crescent homes. There were three homes on each side of it. It had wooden clothes lines going right across it, on which, when necessary, we used to dry tea towels and socks. However when it was cold and we were very reluctant to go out to play, we would creep in there and swing on the 'rads', though always as quietly as possible. This place was really out of bounds except when we were using it as a drying room. There were times when we got caught and a sharp word or two would send us out. We dare not tell Mother and Mr Bangy never told her about us.

Every Saturday evening a gentleman who owned a

watchmakers shop in Clacton used to come round to each house to wind up the clocks, and also of course to change them to winter or summer time. We liked him coming for the summer-time change for it meant we could stay up an extra half-hour. He was also a kindly man and he used to bring a big bag of humbugs to be handed round.

On Sunday mornings we got up at half past seven as only the essential jobs had to be done. This was something I heartily endorsed.

Each Sunday we had to attend one of the four local churches. There was the Baptist Church, the Wesleyan Methodist Church, the Zion Church and Christ Church. None of us particularly liked Christ Church as it was the furthest away and the sermons were tediously long. The Minister was a Reverend J. Alladyce who used to get excited and emotional when delivering his address. In one of his sermons, he suddenly thumped his chest exhorting 'Alladyce, Alladyce! God is calling you!'

When I got home I was sent to bed in disgrace for bursting out laughing at him. Many of the other girls had thought it funny, but unlike me had been able to control their mirth.

The Zionist Church seemed strange to us. However the sermons were short and the people there, although few, were very kind. There was one elderly gentleman in the choir who always gave us a welcoming smile, which we came to look for. I enjoyed going to the Methodist Church. The Reverend L.S. Shutter was a kind and jolly man and at times he would invite us to their social evenings, which we always enjoyed.

The Baptist Church was my favourite. The Minister was the Reverend S.M. Morris who gained notoriety in the local Clacton Times for his stand against cinemas opening on the Sabbath day. In those days we were not even allowed to touch a ball on a Sunday. Our spare time was spent reading a 'Sunday' book, or once a month we wrote to our relatives. I used to write a letter to Miss Goodman. I think that the Reverend Morris was a Welshman. I was fascinated by his speech. He was also very demonstrative in his sermons, but by his oratory, not by making stupid gestures. He held our attention, and most important of all, we understood what he was saying. Many a 'Hear! Hear!' was heard during his sermon. When Mr Cooke (Uncle Ted as he became to me) came down to Clacton during the summer, he always went to the Baptist Church. How thrilled I was when once he came and sat beside me for a morning's service.

On Sunday afternoons we had our own Sunday school. The teachers were local people. I can hear now the Superintendent - a lovely woman- saying 'Bravo!' when we had sung a hymn well. We had our Sunday school anniversary generally on the first Sunday in August, and Uncle used to invite any of the people who came to the Fête Day to come along if they so wished. Each Sunday during the year we were given a card with flowers and a text printed on it. We called them 'Sunday School cards.' At Christmas, we were given a card or calendar; token gifts, but so lovingly given. One Christmas, the Superintendent brought in a big bowl with all the ingredients for a Christmas pudding, and we all went up to the table one by one to have a stir and a wish.

Each year we took part in the Sunday School scripture examinations. These were based on certain stories and characters of the Bible and I always gained a First Prize certificate. For the last year that I was at Groom's the subject was The Life Of Joseph. I was astonished when I not only won a First Prize with Honours, but also the County Prize. Well, I had to excel at something!

5

During the summer holidays, we had a dentist named Mr Jones, who came and stayed at Matron's house for three weeks. This was the amount of time that it took for him to examine and deal with all our teeth. He used to start with Bluebell house and then proceed right through the six Crescent houses. Being in Rosebud, we were always fifth. What trepidation we felt when we knew that Mr Jones had arrived! No gas or cocaine in those days, just 'Open your mouth wider please,' and then 'Ouch!' out it, or they, came. Having seen one girl after another running back home with tears in their eyes and handkerchiefs in their mouths, I was always terrified by the time it came for our house to be done. I knew one girl who had had five out at one time. I remember clinging to the radiators in the waiting room, too frightened to go in, for I could hear the sudden screams and cries emanating from the dentist's room.

This particular year I had promised, after much persuasion, that I would be good. What a relief to them all when I walked meekly into the dental surgery. Well, out came the warning,

'Can you open your mouth a little wider please?'

I looked at the nurse (not in my mind the nicest person at the best of times). I saw a look of triumph on her face that I did not like. How I managed it I will never know, but with one bound I was out of that chair, out of the house and running like mad to the fête ground. The fête ground had tiers of wooden seats like a football stadium, about eight sections high. I bounded up the concrete steps, right to the very top of the furthest corner. The workmen's foreman, Mr Nash, was sent to fetch me. It turned into a game of cat and mouse. As he started to come up the steps towards me, I started to run down a different flight. This had gone on for a while, when suddenly I seized my chance and rushed down the steps past Mr Nash and onto the waste ground. I jumped into the biggest hole in the ground, which was covered in stinging nettles. There I stayed, too frightened to move. Presently, along came Miss Edwards, the Assistant Matron. She called me to her saying that she would not be cross with me, but still I held back. She said she was not coming down after me and getting herself stung, and then added that Mr Jones had finished for the day. I was stung by the nettles all over my arms and legs. I plucked up the courage and went to her. I was taken to matron's office. Mr Jones was sitting in the corner reading the paper and I had to tell him how sorry I was, and that I would have my tooth extracted first thing on Monday morning. This I did, but I had the rest of Saturday and the whole of Sunday to take matters into my own hands. I wriggled and wriggled that tooth until finally, on the Sunday morning before Church, I pulled it out! It really did hurt, but my mind was at rest.

On the Monday morning I went in to see the dentist. I opened my mouth when told, but to everone's surprise, the tooth was gone. I told him that it had come out whilst I was cleaning my teeth. Was he cross! I was sent off home. I was on tenterhooks all day in case Matron sent for me but nothing, not even a caning, was as bad as going to the dentist. With my own children, I took great care to give them a dentist who understood children and who was humane. I suffered agonies when I took them three times a year and never slept the night before they were due to go. As for myself, I am still a coward at the age of eighty.

One lovely and enjoyable thing happened during our summer holidays, which we looked forward to very much. This was our charabanc day and it was usually held on the 15th of August in memory of John Groom's birthday. The only time it was changed, was when it fell on a Sunday or a fête day. Mr Alfred Groom always informed the visitors in his weekly speech in the middle of our fête performances, that the charabanc would be going through Clacton town centre on a particular afternoon, and he asked them to give us a cheer. We used to be given a balloon each, which we waved out of the 'chara' windows, and as we went along we yelled ourselves hoarse, shouting a special 'Hooray!' when going through the town.

Charabanc day started at half past eleven in the morning. We would have a very early dinner and then go to the fête ground and wait for the charabancs to turn up. We then went into the country for a ride, shouting and singing our hearts out. We all knew the current music hall songs and the First World War songs, and would sing anything that came to mind.

After the charabanc ride we would arrive back at the fête ground for a special tea: tinned fruit, jellies, blancmanges, sandwiches and a fancy cake each. We could eat our fill, but we were careful not to over-indulge because the races were to follow. The tea was always partaken in the big shelter of the fête ground. There were prizes for the races: three pence for the first prize, two pence for second prize and a penny if you came third. Each child was given a tube of fruit pastilles for participating. These races would go on until half past eight, when we would all form a circle and sing Auld Lang Syne.

As I write, I again think of all the organisation and selfless time given to us, even in the Depression years, and I marvel at it all.

During the summer, we would sometimes have a picnic in

the garden. This was a grass area surrounded by trees and hedges, cut in two by a path. On a hot day, Mother might suggest that we have our tea in the garden. We enjoyed this, unlike the picnics on the beach, where our sandwiches sometimes got covered in sand. In the mid-thirties we were given a bathing hut at Holland-on-Sea. All the houses had to take it in turns to use it. It was a long walk to Holland-on-Sea, but it was nice to eat our sandwiches without getting sand in them.

At Easter time we were given a hot cross bun on Good Friday, which was treated like a Sunday (except that we did not go to Church). If it was a pleasant day we would go for a walk and my memory of these walks is that it was invariably windy. I remember the song 'Easter Bonnet' being all the rage but I wondered how they could keep their bonnets on with all that wind. Sometimes we would walk as far as the cemetery and once I was shown Winifred's grave, just a small mound and a number. A favourite walk of mine was to the Valley Road. There was a farm there with pigs and I loved to stand at the farm gate watching them. I found it relaxing.

In September, on a Saturday, Mother would take a few of us older girls to a place called Pudney Woods (pronounced as 'pudding'), to go blackberry picking. We would each take a tin, a toffee tin for the younger ones and a biscuit tin for the older girls. It was a long walk so only the girls from eleven years onwards were allowed to go. On the first trip, we would eat far more blackberries than we put in the tins, but when we had collected enough we would make our way home. Mother would then cook what we had collected for tea. I have always liked blackberries, not only for the flavour, but also for the memories that they bring.

A strange thing happened to me one summer holiday when

I was about nine. I was not being very good. I wanted to play with a tiny doll's pram, but not the one that we all shared, as it was made of cane and the wheels did not run properly. I had been told I could not take the tiny pram that I preferred, but I took it, ran down across the Crescent and threw it in the meadow. Walking back across the Crescent I saw a man and woman coming through the gate. They called me to them and asked me my name. I told them shyly and then they asked whether I had a sister. I replied that I had had a sister called Winifred but that she had died.

'That's her,' said the woman excitedly.

'She's just like Rene,' agreed the man.

They told me to go and tell the housemother that my Auntie May and Uncle Will were here. I told them that they would have to ring the front door bell and ran into the back yard, and into the house, shouting,

'You can't send me to bed or smack me, because my auntie and uncle are here.'

The holiday housemother told me not to be so silly and to do as I was told immediately. (Dear Miss Booth was away on her annual three weeks holiday, at a momentous time in my life. How I wish she had been there to share my happiness with me - for I did love her so).

I was aching for the doorbell to ring. It rang! The housemother opened the door and then I heard voices. She directed them over to Matron's house so that she could ascertain whether they really were my relatives. It seemed like years but presently Matron phoned through to say that I was to be got ready in my Sunday clothes to go out with them until six o'clock. Yes, they really were my uncle and auntie, my mother's eldest sister and her husband. They had come on a day's coach trip to Clacton and knowing that I was in a home here, had decided to look for me. The driver of the coach suggested that they try John Groom's. I was taken down to the beach and to the shops, and told that I could choose any toy I liked. They asked if I would like a dolly but I declined, saying I would like a yo-yo. These were very popular at that time as Kellogg's were putting little tin ones into their packets of cornflakes. A school-friend had promised to get me one but now I had one of my own. I chose a red and black one. Then Auntie May and Uncle Will took me to have tea in a restaurant. When I was asked what I would like to eat, I replied 'Shrimps and bread and butter please.'

I had never tasted shrimps in my life before but I had seen people eating them. Thank goodness I liked them. I finished my tea with a couple of fancy cakes as well. I really was having a beano. I was then dying to get back to brag about it to all the other girls. When they returned me to Rosebud house the mother asked my aunt and uncle if they would like to see the dining room. They came in and saw all the girls, and then gave them each a penny. I had a sixpence. No more getting on to me by the older girls now. They all reckoned my relatives were millionaires. My status rose from then on.

A few weeks later, I received a long letter from another aunt, my mother's youngest sister, Beatrice. Aunt Beatrice, Uncle Tom and a cousin Roy, wrote to say that they would be coming down to visit me later on in the year. Eventually they came with Auntie May and Uncle Will, in a car, a very rare thing for ordinary working people to own in those days. They had to go and see Matron again, and once more I was allowed out with them from two o'clock until six o'clock. Butlins had just started a camp at Jaywick Sands and my uncle parked the car near there. Roy and I were playing with a ball when it went bouncing onto a man's table. He had put it outside his tent to have his tea on. He was not very pleased but my aunt soon had things put right. Again these 'millionaires' gave each girl a penny and myself sixpence. At Christmas that year, when the parcels came round on the handcart with Mummy and Daddy Christmas, I had three.

i. Marjorie (left) and twin sister Winifred, 1923.

ii. Marjorie with Miss Booth, 'Mother'

iii. John Groom's Crescent homes, Clacton-on-Sea

iv. Fire drill on fête days

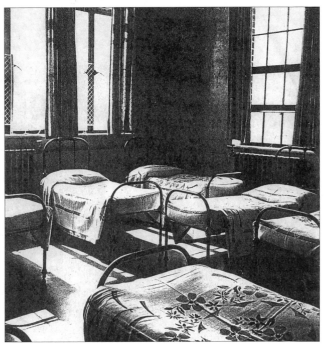

v. A John Groom's dormitory of the 1920s

vi. Mr Alfred Groom who took over from his father and became known to us as 'Uncle'

vii. Mr Cooke, a father figure to me

*viii. The mother I never knew, with my father and
my sisters Rene (standing on the chair) and Ivy*

6

I was four and a half years old when it was decided that I was definitely ready for school. There was a place at the Holland Road School that my friend Phyllis attended, but the school said that I was too young to start yet. When Matron Phillips replaced Matron Wallace (of whom I remember very little except that she seemed a very genteel person) she decided that I needed more discipline, so when I was five years old she sent me to St. Osyth Road School.

The headmaster at Holland Road School, a Mr Read, rarely used the cane on either boys or girls and I knew that the girls who attended Holland Road School seemed to be very happy. The headmaster of St. Osyth Road School was a Mr Learoyd. He was known to be a very strict man, who regularly used the cane on the girls and the strap on the boys; so it was with much trepidation that I started at St. Osyth Road.

It was a large school, which had both infants and seniors. One part of the school, with just four classrooms, was the infants department. It was separated from the senior department by a long corridor, with a door at the end of it leading to the senior school. The senior part of the school had a very large hall, used for assembly, dancing and physical training. Leading off from the hall were the classrooms and there were also a couple of classrooms at each end of the corridors. The furthest corridor led to the headmaster's room. Each classroom had large windows, but the bottom part of each window was blanked out with paint so the children would not be distracted by looking out. The glass panels in the classroom doors were also blanked out, enabling the headmaster to peep over to see if the children were attending to their lessons, but preventing the children from seeing when he was on the prowl. There were times when he caught a child being inattentive and the child would be sent to his room to be caned or strapped. Such was the discipline of the '30s at some schools. When my own children went to school I told them to report to me if any smacking or caning happened to them. It proved unnecessary, but if it had happened to them I would have lost no time in going to the school for an explanation, for you cannot teach children by barbarism.

The infants had a separate entrance into their playground, which was also used by the girls, although the girls had a different play area. The boys' entrance and playground was near the headmaster's room. A high wall separated the boys' and girls' playgrounds. Sometimes we infants had to go and play in the girls' playground and a frequent game of the big girls was to get one of us little ones and jump us up between them, so we could see over the wall and tell them which boys we could see. They would tell us their names and describe them to us so we would not get them muddled up. I enjoyed being jumped up, so I would say that I could see a particular boy even though I had not the foggiest idea who each one was. I was then given another turn so I could tell them more. In fact they preferred me because the other little ones did not seem to be able to spot a particular boy they wanted to know about! Considering that boys and girls left school at fourteen years old, and in those days they were very immature at that age, it was all harmless fun.

Very few went to the Secondary School (the name given in those days to the Grammar or High school) and I suspect that it had little to do with ability. It all boiled down to the fact that most parents could not afford to send their children. I remember that at John Grooms, just two girls went to the Secondary School, Winnie Capon and Joyce Brightmore. Joyce had previously been at a High School before coming to Groom's. I liked her very much. She had personality, was a good dancer and had been to ballet school. Most of all I remember her sitting in the kitchen away from the hubbub of the dining room, doing her homework and being in tears because there was no one to help her. I remember feeling glad that I was not clever. Joyce only remained with us at Clacton for two or three years. I have often wondered what became of her, with her undoubted talents and acting ability, and whether she ever succeeded in gaining a career in that sphere.

In the Infants on Friday afternoons we were allowed to take a toy or game into school, but of course I had none of my own and had to share with someone else who had a toy. I do remember when very young, longing for a doll of my very own; any sort of doll, but especially a rag one if possible. I never had one until the age of twelve when my aunt sent me one, but then I swapped it with one of the younger girls for her Ludo and Snakes and Ladders. What I did have to call my own, once when very young, was a wooden soldier painted red and blue, with a black Busby hat on his head. In the dining room we had two radiators, one either side of the big bookcase, and one cold winters' day I tried to warm my soldier by putting him between the radiator fins. Alas he got stuck; I could see him but no matter how I tried I just could not move him. In fact no one could. I just cried and cried but to no avail. He was well and truly stuck behind the radiator. It was not until years later that one day he suddenly fell down, but his paintwork was completely gone; he was just a piece of wood.

If there was no one to share a game or toy with at school, we were given a piece of cardboard with holes in and a long coloured bootlace which we tried to thread through the holes, like you would when lacing your shoes. Now recalling that, I also recall wearing long boots and the tears and frustrations I experienced when trying to do them up. At first it was long boots with buttons and these were done up with the aid of a buttonhook. Later came the laces. What joy we had when those wretched boots went out of fashion and we just had lace-up shoes. We mostly wore black socks but when we were twelve years old we had black ribbed stockings held up by garters! I remember when very young, wearing white socks with black patent ankle strapped shoes with a little white pearl button in the front. These must have been for best. I also recall wearing for indoors, little ankle strapped slippers with Jack and Jill painted on them. I was very fond of these.

I also remember wearing pure white starched pinafores, stiff as stiff could be, over a host of other clothing. First came the combinations ('coms' for short); then there was the liberty bodice; then a grey flannelette petticoat. Under the petticoat were black knickerbockers, not held up with elastic (those came later) but with two large buttons either side (the type of buttons seen on workmen's overalls years ago). Then came the crème de la crème, a pleated skirt with a white bodice attached to it, and finally a red jumper.

Well, I am digressing a little. Yes, they were very strict at St. Osyth School. In the Infants it was not too bad, but that only lasted until you were eight years old. The caretaker of the school was a big frightening man named Mr Wyatt. He used to shout and threaten us that he would tell Mr Learoyd if we performed any misdemeanour. As I think of that man I can still smell the disinfectant (which was in powder form) that he scattered over the classrooms and corridors when he began to do the cleaning at the end of the day.

The dreaded day came when I was old enough to be put up into the big school. In the big school we had an assembly in the hall every day. At the end of the assembly Mr Learoyd would ask if anyone had dirty shoes on. If you had, you had to wait behind in the hall until he came to inspect them. I remember feeling very guilty one morning, because the previous day had been very wet and it was hard to get a shine on my damp shoes. I stayed behind working myself into a 'tizz' about what I would tell him. He just told me that I had been very honest and I was to go to class. Was I relieved!

At the beginning of the month, a report had to be sent to the House Mistress or Master. We had a house meeting after assembly on the first Monday of each month. We were given a house to be in throughout our whole time at the school. The houses were Romans (red), Trojans (blue), Grecians (yellow) and Spartans (green). After assembly we would march to our different houses, for the monthly meeting, and there a report was read out about individual pupils. What a relief if your name was missed, for if it was read out, it was invariably for some trivial misdemeanour that you had supposedly committed, but which usually you had no memory of doing. I remember one Friday being asked to take the 'reports' across to the head of Trojan House by our form mistress, Miss Everett. When I returned to the classroom she gave me a big apple saying 'Thank you dear,' so on the Monday morning I went quite happily to the house meeting. Surely there was some mistake, for my name was called out and I was told to stand with another girl. For the life of me I could not remember doing anything wrong, but sure enough we then had to go and stand outside the headmaster's room. How we shook, and no wonder, for when our turn came we were told to hold out our hands while Miss Everett gave us the cane. I was now fasy learning to trust nobody.'

I remember a boy in our class by the name of Starling who was desperately poor and who was away from school through lack of footwear. When he did return the next day he wore a very ragged pair of plimsolls. He was sent by the headmaster to his room and given a severe strapping. All my life I have been able to recall the white, starved looking face of that boy, tear-stained through the beating he had just received. I remember feeling so desperately sorry for him, and yes, angry too. I think that unknown to myself at the time, it was then that I became a Socialist. Another incident that influenced my thinking also took place in the early thirties, when we were going back to the orphanage after our Saturday walk. It was getting dusk and across the road was the unemployment exchange, where in a long bedraggled queue, men were waiting to get their dole money. A little girl in our house also looked across the road at that queue and saw her father in it. She was eight years old, and I remember putting my arm around her when one of the other girls said 'Lily, there's your dad.' Poor, poor little mite. We were well dressed and well cared for. John Groom was so right in allowing us to attend the schools provided by the Essex County School Committee, for we saw the life of ordinary people.

On Thursday mornings we had to go to Miss Clark's room for handwork lessons. That meant drawing, cutting out and making things. I was not very good at that. One particular Thursday we had pieces of coloured cardboard handed out to us and we had to make a comb case. Miss Clark used to shout and smack us. I was terrified of her. She came to my desk, looked at my work and 'wallop!' She hit me round my head several times, my head bumping down on the desk each time. I went home to dinner but my head really ached and I did not know what I was doing, so I took myself over to Daffodil. When the sister saw me she put me straight to bed. A short while later Mother came to see me. She came to my bed and said to the sister, 'I hear the teacher hit her.' Turning to me she asked, 'Is that true dear?' I lied and said 'No,' because I was so scared. A while later, Dr Fox, who dealt with all our ailments, called. I was pronounced very ill and moved into a little ward with just one bed in. The ward was next to Sister's bedroom and I received great kindness, not only from sister, but also from her assistant nurse. I was given an umbrella to knock on the wall with in the night, should I need her. I also remember having a glass of orange juice on a locker by my bed, a great luxury indeed!

Well the days went by and I remember very little except that the day before Christmas Eve I was moved into a ward with four beds. I did not realise that it was Christmas time until on Christmas afternoon Mother came over to see me. A box containing presents had been put by my bed, but I had been totally unaware of it. Mother sat by my bed and then proceeded to take the presents out of the box and undo them for me. I remember that my aunt had sent me a pair of real leather gloves. Poor Mum, she was so worried and so kind.

A few days later, lying in bed in the ward, I heard such a commotion. Some new little girls had come to Groom's. Before being allocated to a house, new girls always went to Daffodil, to make sure they were all right, medically and in other ways. The screams were caused by the fear of having a bath. I doubt if these children had ever seen a bath before. After being bathed they were put into my ward. There were two young girls, one a mite of about two years old, but such was the emaciation of her body that she only looked about nine months. Her little legs were like matchsticks; and her sister had marks on her body where her father had strapped her. Talking to me, she said that there were rats in her daddy's house. As I had lived in John

Groom's all my life I could barely believe it, but in a few months time I noticed how bonny they were getting. I wonder how many other children were saved from such degradation and poverty by the work of John Groom's.

One thing I do appreciate about going to St Osyth Road School is that Mr Learoyd taught us to enjoy good music. I very clearly recall sitting in one of the classrooms, listening to the senior pupils singing songs from Gilbert and Sullivan operas. Mr Learoyd belonged to the Clacton Operatic Society, and we were always invited to the shows. I liked the Gilbert and Sullivan operas, but best of all was the year that they did Edward German's 'Merrie England'. That has always been a favourite of mine. How we all loved these shows and I have memories of walking home in the dark afterwards, humming the tunes or softly singing. At school we listened to a lot of music by Handel, and also by Bach - especially Jesu Joy Of Man's Desiring. We had a teacher called Mr Green who played the cello, and another teacher called Mr Taylor who played the piano. A piece of music I loved very much (and I remember Mr Learoyd singing it) was a piece by the French composer Lully, called Sombre Woods. To me it was a really beautiful piece, but it is never heard on the radio. I have written to ask for it to be played, having once heard Owen Brannigan sing it, but that is over forty years ago now.

One day during a singing lesson, Mr Learoyd came into our classroom and told us to sing 'Now Thank We All Our God.' We sang a couple of verses and then he asked if any one of us knew the words to the last verse. Up shot my hand and I recited it to him. He was so pleased that he gave me tuppence (two old pence, but what a lot you could get for that amount). To be honest it was only minutes before the lesson that I had memorised those words, never dreaming that I would be asked to say them. I often used to read verse or poetry between lessons, and also if I could get a copy, the next instalment of our class novel. It was only by reading ahead the story of Treasure Island that I became interested in the book, for it was read to us by a teacher who droned the words out.

We were always invited to the Princess Theatre's plays and productions. On one occasion we were invited to the Christmas pantomime and who should be playing the villain but Mr Learoyd! During the interval we were all given a bag of Mickey Mouse toffees. 'Now,' said the assistant matron, Miss Edwards, 'someone will have to thank them for their kindness.' The villain was walking up and down the aisle, dressed in his costume with green shiny strips of paper across his face, and the lights were just dimming. I was sitting just in front of Miss Edwards and pretended not to hear when the suggestion was made that the person to be chosen should be me; but of course I was quickly made aware of the 'honour' and it was with trepidation that I approached the villain to say my piece. My fear later turned to smiles when an extra bag of toffees were sent down for me, much to the chagrin of Miss Edwards.

In spite of all the strict discipline, I quite enjoyed myself at St. Osyth Road School and it was with some consternation that we heard that a new school had been built at London Road, in place of a little school called the National School that was situated by the Clacton playing fields. All who lived nearer to London Road were to be transferred to the new school, which was to be known as London Road School. The headmaster was to be the former headmaster of the National School. We had never heard of him before, but it is a name many of us will never forget.

This school was opening at the beginning of the summer term and I was first taken to the senior school to see if I could get in there a little earlier. But no, I was to do the one term at London Road School.

I shall never forget the first assembly at that school. Mr Cole, for that was his name, started by introducing himself and the headmistress (whose name at the present I cannot recall, but whose callousness was just as great as his). Then we all had to say good morning to him. He then gave a resumé of the school and ended by saying, 'We have the children from the orphanage here, and let me tell you girls we are having none of your nonsense here. You are going to do as you are told, not be spoilt as you have been at your other schools.' We could not believe our ears. We had done nothing!

Well, I was put in the top class, because the classes just went by age. A Miss Troll was the mistress. I do not remember much about her teaching, except for the incident I am now going to relate. Before we went to the school the prefects were chosen from the children who had been to the National School. One morning Miss Troll had to leave the classroom for a while and she called out the prefect, a Gladys Read. She told her to stand in front of the class to see that no one spoke while she was away. Well no one did speak. We knew that we would be reported if we did. However, when the teacher returned, she asked if anyone had spoken. 'Yes,' said Gladys, and she said it was one of the orphanage girls, and pointed to Mary Nichols who sat just in front of me. I was absolutely incensed. Mary was a quiet girl who would not say 'Boo' to a goose.

'Come out here,' said the teacher.

Mary was really frightened, so I shouted out that she had not said a word.

'Then you come out here then.'

'No,' I said, 'we have done nothing wrong.'

She then came up to my desk, took me by the front of my

hair, and proceeded to pull me to the front. My temper rose. I hit her arm. She let go and ran next door for the headmistress. In she came.

'Come along, lady fair,' she said and pushed up the sleeve of my dress. Then she started to hit me. I hit back. Off she went to fetch Mr Cole. Then came the dramatics. He shouted and literally bellowed at me. Did I know what Borstal was, because he would send me there? By that time I was in a dreadful state. The school caretaker was sent for to see that all the school gates were locked and then to take me to the toilet. He was a kind man and said softly, 'Poor little soul, don't worry,' adding 'The old devil.'

However, he had to take me back to the headmaster's room, and there the three of them were, waiting with the cane and also a bowl of hot water for it to be dipped into before each one in turn administered it to me. I was then sent back to the classroom and told to sit at the back of the class. At dinnertime Miss Troll had been instructed to take me home to Matron Phillips office. The maid let us into the office and then Miss Troll proceeded to tell her what I had done wrong, never of course mentioning that we from Grooms had been wrongly accused of misbehaviour.

'Oh,' said Matron Phillips, 'this calls for a good thrashing.'

Miss Troll, to her credit, said quickly that I had already been severely caned.

'Right,' said Matron Phillips, 'then I shall add to her punishment. For a month, you will come home from school and go straight to bed without any tea.'

In the afternoon of that dreadful day, we had handwork and I was trying to do my work but finding it very hard to hold anything because my hands were so painful. Miss Troll came up to my desk and asked did I want any help. I said 'No.' I would not have taken help from her, or from anyone else at that school even if it had meant another skelping. I hated them all.

As it was summer time, my punishment meant that I could no longer take part in any of the Fête days. I also had to go without my Saturday penny for a month and all 'extras.' The extras were that each Saturday, besides our Saturday penny, we had a piece of fruit of some kind, usually an apple or an orange; and on Sundays we had jam on one of our pieces of bread and a piece of cake.

I was given no opportunity to state the reason why it had all happened in the first place. I must also mention that only two days before my escapade, the headmistress of London Road School had made one of our girls stand in the corner all day in her classroom, and that girl had both legs in callipers! But of course, we dare not say anything. If only we had had Matron Langridge at the time it would have been a different story.

Well, the wonderful day came when I was to leave that dreadful school, but I felt genuinely sorry for the girls that were left there. Years later when visiting Clacton with my own family in the 1960s, I met one of our girls who was living at Clacton and bringing her own children up there. In the course of conversation she mentioned that Mr Cole was still the headmaster of London Road School where one of her children had to go, and she said what a dreadful man he still was. Could such brutality happen today I wonder? I am all for discipline for children, whether at home or school, but sheer brutality - NO!

7

Everyone told me that I would be very happy at the new senior school at Pathfields Road. The headmaster was Mr Read, the former headmaster of Holland Road School. He was a little man in stature (nick-named Jumbo by the boys) but he ruled by having a points system and by making the pupils feel ashamed of their misbehaviour. Each class had a board with all the pupils' names on, and if they misbehaved they would lose a point for their house. Three points in a week meant a good telling off, or in exceptional cases the cane; but I only heard of the cane being used once. To lose three points in a term was considered bad. If you lost a point one week you had to report it to the head of your house. I remember once going to report to the head of Dickens House and she said something that I thought was funny, so she ended up taking off another point herself. Gosh, I remember treading very carefully after that, for the rest of the term. As at St. Osyth's we were given a house to belong to for all the time we were at the school. The houses were Horatio Nelson (red), Charles Dickens (blue), John Ruskin (yellow) and Oliver Cromwell (green). Again, we had monthly meetings, but this time, with no reports from the classrooms. However, we did have to tell the house if we lost any points and the reason why we lost it, or them. These meetings were held at the end of an afternoon, on a day decided by Mr Read. The school was a revelation in the thirties, really progressive.

When new to the school, at the beginning of the school year, we all paraded on the quadrangle. Our names were read out and we were told which form we were to go in. Then we went to our form rooms and were introduced to our form teacher. The teacher gave us each a writing book, which was to be our own personal book for taking notes, etc. At the back of the book we wrote our lessons for each day, the teachers' names and which rooms the lessons would take place in. The week was a seven-day period of schooldays. Monday would be 'day one', one week but 'day six' the following week, with Wednesday becoming the new 'day one'. This not only helped to get all the subjects in, but it also made the week more interesting and in my view stimulated a zest for learning. The most important thing was that we were being treated like responsible young people. That alone made a difference to our personal well-being.

Each classroom was used for a different subject. The history room had displays of the different ages, of the monarchs, and of periods such as the Industrial Revolution. The geography room likewise, had maps and pictures of different countries. There was a projector used for both films and slides. The art and craft room had looms and various paraphernalia, with two sinks in it for mixing colours or washing brushes. The science room you could not mistake for all the cages around the room containing a variety of different species of small animals. At the back of the room were the cages with mice in them. Ugh! How I dreaded the thought of any of them escaping, but they never did. No, science was definitely not for me! We also had a big cookery room with plenty of utensils and three or four cookers. The boys had a large woodwork room and I imagine that the school turned out many a good carpenter. There was also a well-equipped needlework room, which was also used for hygiene lessons and home nursing. These last two subjects I found very interesting, but not needlework.

My very favourite room was the music room. There was a grand piano in one corner, and in the far corner a big electric gramophone. What beautiful records were played on it by Miss Brown: music by Handel, Bach, Schubert, Tchaikovsky and Grieg. A favourite piece of mine has always been the Allegro from Grieg's piano concerto in A minor. I loved those music lessons although I was never able to learn to play any instrument. I am so happy to think that our grandchildren can. Apart from singing, listening to and learning to read music, we also had one lesson in the ordinary classroom where we were taught to write down pieces of music.

Some of the classes were situated around the quadrangle, which was under cover so that we could be sheltered from the inclement weather. It was indeed a revolution in schooling at that time and how lucky we were to go to such a happy school. Assemblies were held each morning. The school was divided into two halves and each half went to assembly on alternate mornings. The mornings that you did not go to assembly were used for scripture lessons. I always came top for scripture, music and English, and one year I surprised not only myself but the teacher too, when I came top for cookery. It was a mere fluke for I did not care for the subject very much. I think I must have excelled at the theory! At the end of the year we had examinations and reports. We each had our own individual report book, which we kept throughout our years at the school. The school uniform was blue and gold and the report book was blue with gold lettering. I kept mine for years.

Whichever school we in Groom's attended, we always wore the school uniform, and very smart we looked at Pathfields Road, with our white blouses, pleated gymslips and blue and gold ties. We also had velour hats displaying the school badge. Later, the hats were discarded in favour of berets, but they also had the school badge on them. We had black lace-up shoes and black stockings. Our overcoats were navy blue, and very warm with deep pockets. I remember in the early years having to have my pockets sewn up because of the numerous things I carried in them, like a top, marbles, and string. We were told just to keep our gloves in them, but I was always losing mine. For some reason or other I hated wearing gloves and to this day I never wear them. In the summer we had blue dresses with gold beading down the front and around the sleeves. Our footwear was white socks and brown sandals. All our clothes such as dresses and blouses were made by Miss Fitt and Miss Church, who were very hard-working and nice people.

During the summer holidays, Matron Phillips used to set aside one afternoon to have us all go to the 'Sanny' to hear some of the school reports read out, and if yours was not good you would be told off in front of all the other girls. One year I had a bad report. At that time, Mr Cooke was staying for a few extra days at Clacton and was shown my bad report. Mother received a telephone call to say that I was to go over to Matron's office because Mr Cooke wanted to see me. Mother made me put on my best Sunday clothes and my panama hat, and I went skipping over to see Mr Cooke. When I got there I was shown very curtly into a room and told to stay there. Noticing the attitude of the maid I thought, 'Oh, Matron Phillips doesn't like me being favoured to see Mr Cooke.' I was told to take off my panama hat with the words, 'You're not going anywhere.'

'Funny,' I thought. I decided to tread very warily when I was let into the room to see him. It was just as well that I did. Into the office I went. Matron's first words to me were, 'You can take that smile off your face at once. You should be getting a good smacking.' Mr Cooke put up his hand to stop her.

'Come here my dear,' he said, and put his arm around me.

'Now,' he said, 'You haven't done very well have you?' He had my report book in front of him. 'Don't you like arithmetic?' he asked.

'No, I'm not very good at it,' I said.

'Well,' he said, 'will you try hard to like it for me? It says here that you have ability but do not try. Can you try for me?'

'Yes,' I replied.

The following term I came second in class, and by the end of that school year I had come top. I went about with a smug look on my face, dying for the afternoon when Matron would have us congregate in the 'Sanny' for the reports to be read. Needless to say, she did not read out any reports that year! By the time I was thirteen I really wanted to learn, but we had to leave school at fourteen. I was very upset when the time came for me to go.

One punishment we had at school, if we were caught talking in class or if we got behind with our work, or hadn't done it correctly, was to be given detention. I wasn't keen on this, especially in the wintertime, as I was inclined to be scared of the dark. If it happened to be the 5th of November then that would be a calamity, for at John Groom's, whatever National celebration there was, we always took part in it. We would dash home from school, get our tea as quickly as possible and then we would all crowd on top of the play-cupboard to look out of the window at the marvellous display that the workmen put on for us.

They had two big ladders, and in between, half way up the ladders, was a very long plank on which the fireworks would be displayed. These included Catherine Wheels, and all sorts of other spectacular fireworks. Just the very oldest of the girls were allowed to go out and hold some of the fireworks, but I was quite happy to stay indoors. I didn't like the 'jumping crackers'.

We had a wonderful time. We used to tell some of our friends from school to come along and watch, for some of their parents couldn't afford to buy fireworks for their children, and we felt sorry for them.

8

Each morning, after we had completed our various jobs and we had had our breakfast, the tables were cleared and the Bibles handed out. Mother would read a passage to us and then we had a weekly text to memorise. After this we got ready for school and walked across to the 'Sanny' for a hymn and a prayer with Matron. This latter idea was only carried out when we had our new matron, Matron Langridge. She was a lovely woman. If only she had been our matron for all those other years instead of Matron Phillips and Miss Edwards (her deputy). Matron Langridge had a maid called Lucy. She was very nice too and she adored Matron Langridge. We all did. She was strict, but jolly and very fair. She had a keen sense of humour and always knew when to turn a blind eye.

As for Matron Phillips and Miss Edwards - what a pair! Very few of the girls liked them, and most were terrified of them. I was too, but I was determined not to show it. Every Sunday morning when the girls with their house mothers had paraded on to the Crescent ready for church, Matron Phillips came over to see each section and to have a word with the mother before we started off. (A memory I have is of how beautifully dressed we were, with the younger ones in their flowered dresses and flower-bedecked hats, and us older ones in our panama hats).

However, one Sunday she noticed that I was not there. I had been sent to bed for kicking another girl under the table (a regular practice if a disagreement started at the table, but I had been found out). When Mother and the other girls returned from church, Matron Phillips came over to the house on the pretence that she wanted to see the dormitory windows and curtains. She came into the dormitory and looked at the windows, and then she turned to the Mother and said, 'Is this little girl ill?'

'No,' replied Mother, 'I have sent her to bed for being naughty.'

'Oh, I see.' She came and sat on my bed and said, 'Little girls like you deserve a good spanking, ' and she began to clap her hands like mad.

Then she got up to walk out of the door and as she went I yelled at her, 'Daft fool!' Back she came. She pulled back the bedclothes and tried to lift up my nightdress to give me a good thrashing. Like a young fiend I fought her, flaying my arms and legs all over the place. She did not succeed and eventually went downstairs telling the rest of the girls to send me to Coventry. One of the house-girls said that it was cruel, and before the day was out had been moved from Rosebud into a different house. I then felt sorry for her as the other house had a stricter mother. After this episode we knew that the wretched woman would get back at us somehow.

Shortly afterwards there was an epidemic of scarlet fever. Each house was systematically fumigated under the instruction of Matron Phillips. Whilst our house was being done we were all banished to the holiday home which adjoined Snowdrop, Matron's house. The other Mothers stayed with the girls, but not our mum. The poor woman had to go and live in Snowdrop. I remember seeing her walking by the window and we would rush up to it and call out, 'When are we all going back to Rosebud?' She dare not stay and talk to us and there were tears in her eyes. Like us she was very unhappy, for we all loved her. Those days in quarantine stand out in my mind for we were not allowed to go to school either. Phyllis, my special friend through all the time I spent at Grooms, had been infected with the fever. I remember going into her cubicle and kissing her goodnight but then gargling furiously with salt water. I never got it, but Phyl was taken to the Clacton Isolation Hospital.

Eventually the crisis passed, although it seemed ages to us. Just as we thought everyone was clear we were invited to see 'The Gondoliers' at the Princess Theatre. We were very excited at the prospect of going. At last everything would be back to normal! At the very last minute we were put back into quarantine. I cannot express in words how devastated we all were. We were so looking forward to it and we never got another chance to go.

At about the end of November we were back in a house again. However, Matron decided to separate us all. I was put in Pansy with Miss Booker who was really the Mother for Mignonette. We thought that she would be quite nice, but she was not half as nice as Miss Booth. She expected us to be little angels. Well, she must have been disillusioned!

One incident occurred at Christmas. After Christmas Day and Boxing Day it was back to reality. It had not seemed like Christmas, as there had been no build-up and no Mum whom we loved. We were a bit down in the mouth and so decided to cheer ourselves up a bit. We would do a show with different sketches and things. We had done a few but no one seemed very happy so I said that I had thought of a good one. I hurried out of the room and went to the beetle cupboard to dress up. The beetle cupboard was the cupboard under the stairs, which housed the old dresses and the aprons we used for doing our various jobs. I put on some of these old clothes and then got some soot from the kitchen chimney and blacked my face. I went in and sang 'Sonny Boy.' There were howls of laughter and in the middle of my act Miss Booker walked in to see what all the noise was about. She was horrified to say the least. Did I want to grow up as a poor little black boy in Africa? I should be ashamed of myself! We were so surprised at her reaction as we were only having a bit of fun. We thought that Mum (Miss Booth) would have seen the funny side. She would probably have called me a 'Ninny' but we would all have laughed.

I cannot recall much of living in Pansy, only that we disliked it. We were all feeling so insecure - a terrible thing I think, for a child.

A few months later I was transferred to Lily. There I was extremely unhappy. I cannot remember who the Mother was, only that she had a cockney accent. I used to imitate her and so I was sent over to Matron. This called for drastic punishment and I was sent over to Daffodil to live with Sister Forbes. She was said to be very strict which she was, but behind that exterior was a kind heart and most important to me, a sense of humour. She also liked good music and on Saturday nights I used to lie in bed and listen to the 'Henry Wood Proms'. She did not realise it, but I remember how much I used to enjoy listening to them. In those days there were just the National and Regional stations. During this time I also became quite proficient at darning. As fast as I mended the socks she would pull them apart again. This was all part of my punishment. If they were white socks I had to do all the warp threads with cotton and all the weft with wool.

One Sunday we had to go to an afternoon service at the Baptist Church. In the middle of the service (which was conducted by the Sunday School Superintendent who happened to be our school's science master) we were told that as we sang the next hymn we were to think about the words and then go out to the front to sign the pledge. Everyone trooped out to sign, but partly from bravado and partly because I did not know if I would be able to keep it up when I got older, I refused to sign. When I got back to Daffodil, Matron was sitting with Sister Forbes, and she asked me about the service. I told her that we had been asked to sign the pledge. Then she asked me whether I had signed. I thought, 'Now I am really in trouble.'

'Why didn't you sign?' asked Matron. I answered that I did not know if I would be able to keep it up. She told me that I had been quite right. At the Sunday evening service the girls were reprimanded for signing the pledge without giving themselves time to think about it. I was then held up as a 'Paragon of Virtue' and the girls lost no time in letting me know. As a consequence I was returned to Lily house, my punishment ended.

Back in Lily house I found a different Housemother, a Miss Walmsley. She was a nice capable person and the house had an air of restfulness about it. Everyone seemed to know their duties and just got on with them. Although Miss Walmsley was a quiet sort of person, her authority was strong and we all respected her. I had a friend in that house called Jessica Griffiths. We were about the same age and were due to leave school at the same time. Because of the easy discipline and the well-ordered house that Miss Walmsley had created I was looking forward to being a house-girl there, but my luck was out.

When I was fourteen and had just left school, Miss Walmsley called me into her sitting room one day and told me that Matron had a special job for me and that she wanted to see me immediately. I must admit that I was loath to go and that it was with great trepidation that I packed my clothes and went over to see Matron. She explained to me that she was going to use Violet house as a 'Tweenies' home for the children between the ages of five and seven. The head of the house would be a

Miss Reed and a Miss Beeton would also help her, along with myself and another house-girl. We were given a small bedroom downstairs for the two of us.

As soon as I walked into that house I had a strange feeling. I cannot explain it to this day, but I had a feeling of great misgivings. We had to see to the children but most of the work was what I would term as 'donkey work'. I never saw Miss Reed or Miss Beeton doing anything particular. All the cleaning and washing up had to be done by us two. In the dining room there were four long tables with one of us sitting at the head of each table. We were totally responsible for the children sitting at our table, including their manners. What I encountered in that house was gross cruelty to some of those little ones. Miss Reed had her favourites and Heaven help those who were not. She would thrash those children for no real misbehaviour. One incident has remained in my mind all my life. At my table one day I thought I had surreptitiously told one of my children to hold her spoon correctly, but Miss Reed had obviously heard. She dashed up to the table, grabbed the child from her chair and started to severely smack her. To this day I recall how I felt for that little girl and what I had unwittingly caused to be done to her. I was in tears; the little girl was so helpless and in no way deserved that harsh treatment. I was then ordered into the shoe room to clean all the shoes by myself. I overheard Miss Reed on the telephone, presumably to Matron, saying that she was not happy with me and that I was unsuitable for the job. If I have ever really loathed anyone in my life it has been that dreadful cruel woman. How she was never found out beats me. Years later when I was in the W.A.A.F. Uncle Ted sent me photo as a reminder of John Grooms in earlier years, with himself and the little ones. On the same photograph with him and the children was Miss Reed, so I just tore the photograph up.

From Violet, the Tweenies house, I was sent back to Daffodil to live once again with Sister Forbes. I was then sent to work in the large communal kitchens with Mrs Webb, our head cook. She had two local ladies to help her, called Joyce and Betty. Joyce was all right, but Betty was very popular with us all. She had a very kind and efficient way with her.

The first thing that I had to do in the mornings was to help Joyce and Betty to prepare the potatoes. Before that though, Mr Kent would come in and put all the potatoes in a huge peeler. He would turn the big wheel and all the time he was working he would whistle the latest tunes. This I think was for the benefit of Joyce and Betty who at times would laugh, but sometimes would become irritated. When he thought that they were peeled enough he would tip the potatoes into a massive wooden sink, and then Joyce, Betty and I would complete the cleaning of them and transfer them to the huge saucepans. Then there were all the other vegetables to prepare and the sinks and tables had to be scrubbed. They had to be spotlessly white. On occasions, Mrs Webb would call me over to the huge stove to stir the semolina or rice. She would invariably have all the big saucepans at the front of the stove and I would have to reach right over them to do the stirring, which would cause my arms to feel very hot. If Betty asked me to do any stirring she would always make sure that the smaller saucepans were right at the front.

I hated working in the kitchens. On Saturdays the outer kitchen had to be scrubbed. This room contained two coppers in which the custard was made and I had to clean these out too. The thought of thick, cold custard is abhorrent to me to this day. There was also a big skip, containing various things, which I had to pull out of the corner each Saturday when I went to scrub the floor. It was a pale wooden floor and when I pulled out the skip, whitish looking crickets would jump out. The first time that I encountered them, I gave a scream. I was told off, so I dare not scream again, though many was the time that I wanted to. I loathed doing that part of the floor, although I did not mind scrubbing the middle of it, for it came up white very easily.

On Sunday mornings I did not have to go down to the kitchens until ten o'clock, but I had the extra job of sweeping the downstairs wards in Daffodil. This was like a big conservatory in which the ladies from Edgware were put if they were taken ill on one of their holidays at the Holiday Home. These were the crippled ladies and girls who lived and worked at Edgware, London. They lived in houses all named after trees such as Willow, Chestnut, Larch, Elm and Walnut, and they worked making artificial flowers.

One charabanc day, instead of the usual celebrations, we were taken from Clacton to Edgware in Middlesex, to see the new Crippleage of John Grooms. We arrived at about one o'clock in the afternoon and were taken on a tour of the workrooms to see the women making the artificial flowers. I noticed that one of the women had a paintbrush in her teeth, to paint the petals. She had no arms. Some had only one arm, others had crippled legs and some had to wear callipers. They all seemed so happy and excited that we were visiting them. One lady took me with her to see one of the houses and her own private room. She was so thrilled with it. Yes, they were all so happy and took great pride in their new premises, which were a tremendous improvement on Sekforde Street. In each house they had a large communal room to gather in if they wanted to, although their individual rooms were spacious enough for them to read or write in. There was also a cosy kitchen, especially equipped so that they could easily use it.

Again, there was a Housemother in charge. The one at Willow House, a Miss Allard, I got to know very well, but that was to come later on in my life. After seeing the workrooms, we went into a huge hall to have lunch with them. Afterwards, not to be denied our pleasures, we had our games and races on the green.

It was a very lovely and most rewarding day, making us, young as we were, realise that there were others who through the work of John Grooms were finding happiness and fulfilment in their lives. They were learning to earn their own living and because of the facilities provided for them, achieving independence. After all these years, as I sit here recalling the work of John Grooms, I feel humbled and over-awed at the tremendous work and thought that has gone into helping people less fortunate than others. To think that one ordinary young man's goodness could have achieved so much!

However, back to the kitchens. As I have said, I hated working in them, and when Mr Cooke the principal came down for the Tuesday Fête day, I begged him to ask Matron (Mrs Langridge) to take me out of the kitchens and to let me go back into Rosebud with Miss Booth. Well the blessed day came at last, and at the end of September 1937 I was placed back in Rosebud. Was I pleased!

I became a house-girl with my friend Phyllis and in spite of the hard work and responsibilities, they were very happy days indeed.

9

There were always two house girls and seniority depended on age. For a whole year we had to help Mother. It was really training for going into service when we left John Groom's.

On alternate weeks we were either the 'kitchen' girl or the 'dining room' girl. The first job of the kitchen girl was to take Mother her morning cup of tea, and then prepare breakfast for all the girls. We usually had porridge that had to be cooked slowly in the steamer the night before and then reheated in the morning. On Tuesdays we had fried bread, on Saturdays we had bacon, which was always done in a dish in the oven (never fried). On Sundays we had a boiled egg. I could not abide boiled eggs as they made me ill, so Mother used to give me bacon instead. With all our breakfasts we had slices of bread and dripping, two or three slices until thirteen years of age, and then four slices (two whole rounds) at fourteen. This bread had to be cut and prepared by the kitchen house girl.

On Mondays both house girls had to clean the long bay windows and scrub the linoleum floors of the dormitories. On Tuesdays we washed the girls' pinafores and ironed them. In those days we had to put the heavy irons to heat on a gas ring. We would take them off the gas ring and spit on them or hold them to our faces to gauge the temperature. We had two irons to work with, one on the gas ring whilst the other was in use, swapping them over when the first iron got too cool to use. It was a long tedious job.

Wednesday was the day for the kitchen girl to clean Mother's bedroom and for the dining room girl to clean Mother's bathroom. Then the laundry baskets came and we had to check that all items had been returned and note whether any needed repairing. One basket contained all the bed linen and tablecloths. The beds were changed every week, but only the bottom sheet - the top sheet would be moved to the bottom. The other basket held the clothes: vests, knickers, liberty bodices and school blouses. All those buttons! They were forever coming off. In the summer they also contained the school summer dresses. Of course all the older girls hated Wednesday mending night, because as I mentioned before, we were all in charge of one of the little ones, and that meant mending their clothes. I would often offer to scrub the scullery floor if the person whose turn it was to do it would mend a hole or sew a button on for me. I loathed needlework of any kind and would often prick the girl I had to look after for getting a hole in her sock. (Years later at a John Groom's reunion, she reminded me of this).

On Thursdays the kitchen girl had to clean out Mother's sitting room. What a fiddly job it was. I never minded polishing the floor but dusting the ornaments always felt like prying, as they seemed rather personal things to me. The dining room girl had to turn out the dining room, which was a large room with seven big windows. In addition to this she had to take the children to school. The dining room girl, along with two other older girls had to polish the dining room floor every Wednesday and Saturday evening. All forms and chairs were upended onto the tables so that the floor could be thoroughly swept. Then the polishing began. The floors were made of red clay and we used a red tile polish. To get a shine we first rubbed across the floor with our polish rags in our hands. This got the worst of the polish off. Then we put the rag under one foot and went to and fro to get a shine. It was hard work and sometimes, if

Mother was securely in her sitting room and the younger children were in bed, we would put the rag under our bottoms and get another girl to pull us up and down the room. Invariably there would be such high jinks going on, and such hilarity. Although we tried not to be too noisy Mother sometimes caught us. Sometimes we would hear her coming and by the time she opened the door, we would all be dutifully polishing in the proper way, on our hands and knees.

On a Friday the kitchen girl would have to turn out the kitchen. What a job! In the kitchen there was a huge dresser. All the crockery had to be washed and then the cutlery cleaned with bath-brick, or 'brick-dust' as we used to call it. The pot board under the dresser held a variety of utensils: saucepans, steamers, frying pans and different sized kettles. All of these were black and had to be black-leaded. Also the kitchen fireplace and the red tiles of the hearth had to be polished, and of course that the black stove also had to be thoroughly black-leaded. Finally there was a big window and a table the length of the kitchen to be scrubbed. It had drawers at each end, in which we kept the tablecloths and the cutlery. This was the table on which we did the ironing. After this we had to scrub the floor and then polish it. Leading off from the kitchen was the pantry, where we kept the big loaves of bread. Every other day we would take a big wooden tray over the road to the communal kitchens, to collect half a dozen loaves of bread. What a weight they were to carry, and the wooden tray was no lightweight either.

At four o'clock each weekday, the children had to be fetched from school by the dining room girl, while the kitchen girl went to cut the bread and prepare the tea.

Saturdays meant turning out the pantry before going to fetch the bread. There were three wide shelves, which went all the way round the pantry walls. They held three big green tins, one for tea, one for cocoa and one for Demerara sugar. We always had cocoa for breakfast. These tins contained the supplies for the week, but there were some smaller tins, which contained Mother's commodities. All the shelves had to be scrubbed and the tins washed. One of the workmen, a Mr Jack Kent would come to each house with a big handcart to collect the tins, and then return them when they had been refilled. He lived at Woodbine Cottage, which adjoined the 'Sanny.' We all liked him. He was always whistling so he was nicknamed 'Mr Whistler.' On the top of the outside wall of his house was a big black clock. You could see it from every house and quite a way up the road too. It had big gold figures and hands. We very often checked the time by it when the two o'clock hooter went for the workmen to return from their dinner. I think that Mr Kent saw to the winding of it for the works must have been in his house.

Our milkman was a man we nicknamed 'Mr Smiler.' He was a lovely man and very courageous. One day when the brake taking some of the girls to Holland Road School seemed to be in imminent danger of crashing, Mr Smiler put his milk cart in between the two vehicles to try and prevent a worse crash than there would have been. The Clacton Times reported that he certainly saved our girls from injuries. Everybody was full of praise for Mr Smiler, but all he said was that he did not want to see any of the girls hurt.

Whether you were the kitchen house girl or the dining room house girl, each had its advantages and drawbacks. It was hard work but good training. We were given four pence (4d) a week. During the week we had the afternoons off from two o'clock to four o'clock.

When Phyllis had to leave and go into service, a girl called

Elizabeth became the new house-girl with me and fortunately we worked very well together. But my time for leaving Grooms was drawing near.

I had loudly proclaimed that I was not going to clean anybody's floors or wait on them hand and foot, especially if they were able-bodied and able to do it for themselves. I heard Mr Cooke talking to Mother in her room and asking, 'What are we going to do about Marjorie?'

During the years following my first meeting with them, I received several letters from my aunts. One letter from Aunt Beatrice told me that I had a brother Harry and that he was now living with her. Some time later, Harry and his fiancée Doris came down to Clacton to see me. I was allowed out with them and Harry asked me what I was going to do once I had left Grooms. I replied that I did not want to go into service (and he said that no sister of his would). I then told him that if possible I would like to work in an office. This sounded quite 'posh' to me although I was completely naïve about the world and what working in an office would require. He told me not to worry and that he would see what he could do. However, events soon took over. Miss Booth had to go away suddenly to a sick sister and a Mrs Merryweather was sent to look after us for a few days. On one particular afternoon we were taken down to the beach. It was the beginning of April 1938.

The girls were playing with a ball (pig in the middle). Audrey, one of the little girls, had just caught the ball when Mrs Merryweather said, 'Put the ball down. You can't play. You wet the bed this morning.' That absolutely infuriated me. Up I jumped, grabbed the ball, pushed it into the sand and sat on it saying, 'If she can't play with it no one is going to.' I just felt that it was wrong to treat Audrey so. She always looked such a thin, white-faced weak little child to me and I felt very sorry for her. Miss Booth would never have treated the child so. That action of mine of course meant trouble, and when we got home Mrs Merryweather started to jab at me, poking me into the bushes as I tried to get away from her. I stood enough of it and then suddenly burst out, 'Leave me bloody well alone!' That did it! Over to Matron she hurried and I was sent to bed in disgrace. For two days no one was allowed to speak to me.

Two days later I received word that I would be leaving Grooms the following Monday. Mr Cooke had got in touch with my Aunt Beatrice, with whom my brother Harry was living. Harry, I understand, signed papers claiming me, and it was decided that I would live with my Aunt Beatrice, Uncle Tom, Cousin Roy and Harry.

10

I feel I must write a few separate lines about both Matron Langridge and Mr Cooke, two people whom I admired tremendously.

Matron Langridge

After Matron Phillips and Miss Edwards left John Groom's we had a Matron Brown, but she didn't stay very long. Then came Matron Langridge, for my last year at Groom's. We understood that she had previously been the Matron at Edgeware. The first thing she did was to come around to each house to introduce herself to us all and I noticed that Mum looked quite pleased and happy; and well she might for a transformation began to take place.

To start with, when on a Saturday morning the Mothers had to go over to Matron's office, they now, with Matron Langridge, went quite happily. I remember myself, years before, going through agonies of fear when Mother went over to see Matron Phillips. I particularly remember that at one time, I had to clean the bathroom. The walls on either side of the bathroom window held double peg rails, on which we hung our towels and flannels. Of course when hung up they had to be folded neatly and I remember very clearly how I had watched Mum prepare to go over to see Matron Phillips, with the 'Black Book' in her hand. The black book was Matron Phillips idea, and the Mother used to have to put our names in the book if we had been naughty. After the Mothers had been over to see

Matron they would then return to say that either Matron or Miss Edwards wanted to see you because 'your name had been in the book that week' and we all knew what that meant! Luckily, I never had to go, but on this occasion I stood in the bathroom tidying and re-tidying those towels, counting and counting them until Mother came back, dreading all the time that she might say that Matron or Miss Edwards wanted to see me. The girls at Groom's all thought of me as a 'don't care girl'. I did care, though I kept it all to myself, showing a brazen front to all. But those Saturdays of fear remain firmly in my mind.

Now, in later years, I realise that I was almost having a nervous breakdown, for I did suffer terrific nightmares too; waking up petrified and feeling the sweat pouring off me with fear. But I was determined to keep it to myself and overcome it. No one had any inkling about it at all, and I was glad that I had the strength of character to overcome it in the end.

However, I must return to lovely Matron Langridge. The first thing I became aware of about her was that she treated us all as individual people, not to be talked down to, but to talk with. It was significant to hear her talk of her maid Lucy, who she introduced to us as her helper and friend. I know that Lucy loved her, you could see it in her face, and Lucy was always nice to us, and she would say 'hello' if she saw any of us.

Soon after Matron Langridge came, we started having much better meals, although I couldn't really complain before. We had always been extremely well looked after, and going to the ordinary council schools we saw children nowhere near as well dressed or healthy as us. Never-the-less Matron Langridge did give us especially nice food. For instance each day now began with cornflakes, not just bread and dripping. Sunday breakfasts began with grapefruit segments. We also had fruit salads and many other meals unknown to us before.

One memorable thing that she did was to treat the house-girls as adults. First of all she thought that we should be dressed in more grown up clothes. Years before when a girl was leaving Groom's, invariably to go into service, they were 'kitted out' with what we termed as their going away clothes. First of all they were taken out to buy their big case. Then they were given their first two sets of ladies underwear, two dresses, a winter coat, hat, two sets of maids clothes and morning and afternoon wear. They were also given gloves and an umbrella; in fact all that they required to start a new life.

Matron Langridge thought that as we became house-girls, it would be nice for us to have an afternoon dress, a special dress for Sundays, grown-up underwear, coats, hats, etc. So one day we all went into Clacton town to the different shops, to choose our own new outfits. We were also given a big suitcase and an umbrella. In fact, we were treated like little ladies. I know that we were very elated at all these changes, and felt very important. It gave us a status. How right she was, for it gave us a new pride in being house-girls.

After all this 'kitting out' she had another brilliant idea. Most maids had a holiday each year, so she thought 'Why not the house-girls?' Half of us went to Southend-on-Sea and stayed at board residences. Mr Cooke saw us all safely to our different places. I remember that he was staying at Westcliffe for a few days, no doubt to see that all was right with us. We stayed on holiday for two weeks and during our stay we were taken to the theatre and places of interest. I enjoyed it, but I missed Clacton!! When we returned, the other house-girls then went on their holiday. All this shows how caring and thoughtful Matron Langridge was; how she was constantly thinking of our quality of life and also preparing us for the outside world.

One very sad thing occurred in the late summer of 1937,

and although I am recording it, I put no blame on John Grooms or Matron, for no-one could have foreseen such a tragedy.

As I have stated earlier, when the Mothers went on their holidays, we had what we called a 'Holiday Mother.' For me, at a very young age, it was a Godsend, bringing to us in Rosebud House our dear Miss Booth. Unfortunately, this year it backfired. Each mother had either a Wednesday or a Thursday afternoon and evening off each week, and in her capacity as a relief, our new Holiday Mother had to come around to the different houses to see if everything was alright. Although you may feel that I am writing this with hindsight, I am telling the truth when I state that not only us in Rosebud giggled about her, but also, the girls in the other houses mentioned that she seemed a bit strange.

Well one morning, when Mr Polly got to work and went to his greenhouse, the poor man discovered a child's body under some wood, which he had left outside the greenhouse. The child's name was Jenny, and she had come to Grooms in mysterious circumstances. We were told she had been left on the doorstep. Matron Langridge called us all to assemble in the 'Sanny' and she told us in as careful a way as she could, what had happened to little Jenny. It transpired that the Holiday Mother had killed her by throwing her out of the window. Matron Langridge asked us not to mention it at all, but she did warn us that we would most likely hear gossip, which we should ignore. Needless to say, no one said a word, but I recall that when I took the little ones to school one week, there were great big banner headlines on the news placards, saying that at the trial she had admitted to doing it deliberately. She was sent to Broadmoor. Matron Langridge was extremely upset, as anyone could imagine, and we all felt very much sympathy for her.

However, nice things, as you have read, happened too.

During the holiday period we always had open Sunday school. In the middle of one Sunday afternoon there was a commotion outside and suddenly the door opened and in walked these people. We did not know who they were and matron went and spoke to them. She seemed very pleased and invited them in. One man went to the piano and started to play, and then the other two men sang, not hymns as we expected, but songs like 'Mama's Little Baby Likes Shortening Bread.' We joined in, but with our strict religious upbringing we could not help feeling that it was sacrilege to sing anything other than hymns on a Sunday. The people were Derek MacCulloch, the presenter of Children's Hour in the '30s and some of his friends, one of whom was Owen Brannigan. How we enjoyed it all.

So many little treats used to be given to us, and with matron Langridge there was a different atmosphere all over Grooms. In fact it was a very happy place for all concerned.

Several years later, at our centenary reunion, I met Matron Langridge again and from then on kept in contact with her. If ever we had to travel up to the north, on pleasure or duty, both my husband Ernest and I would always make a point of making our way to Harrogate to see her. Ernest thought that she was a most interesting and lovely person. One thing that Matron Langridge said to us was 'My friends call me Nan. Will you?' I felt it was a great honour to be thought of as one of her friends.

Mr Edward Cooke

In 1933, Mr Edward Cooke became the Superintendent of John Groom's, previously having shared the duties of Superintendent and Secretary with Mr Alfred Groom (the son of John). Later he became the Principal. How we all loved that warm-hearted man!

Each Monday in the summer, when he was due to come to

Clacton, we would watch out for him with bated breath. He drove an Austin Morris car and I can still remember the number plate to this day: DXN 633. We would vie with each other to ask if we could clean and polish his car.

We knew that on that Monday evening we would get a visit from him. If we were in bed he would come up to the dormitory and sit on a bed, and we would all gather round him while he chatted to us. We would all chorus, 'Tell us a story!' The lovely man must have been so tired with all the travelling, but he would tell us just one, in spite of our pleadings for more. In the wintertime he came less frequently to Clacton but again he would always make a point of visiting each house. Sometimes Mum would invite us into her sitting room where a lovely fire was burning. Uncle Ted (as we came to call him) would be sitting in an armchair and we would sit on the floor at his knee. Once again came the inevitable request for a story. Sometimes we would say, 'Tell us a sad story,' and he would make up a story about a fellow called Pappymondus who turned out to be a stupid fellow doing all the wrong things, and in the end we would all be laughing our heads off.

When Uncle Ted came to the house it was like a big warm feeling pervading everywhere. When he left, we all felt empty, but his lovely personality and warmth penetrated our hearts and we would always remember what he had said.

One Christmas, Elizabeth and I (the two house-girls) were each given an autograph book. Elizabeth asked Uncle Ted to write in it for her, and when he came back the following week he gave it back to her. Wasn't she happy! He had written her a poem about the 'lovely lady Elizabeth'.

'Gosh!' I thought, 'If he writes something like that about her, what WOULD he write about me?' So I asked him if he would sign my autograph book. He duly took it away and when he returned he handed it back to me, going swiftly into Mother's sitting room. Eagerly I opened it, and I can remember to this day what he wrote:

'What I see in Marjorie, for whom I have a great regard. I see the making of a very fine woman who everyone will be pleased to know.'

'That's fair,' I thought.

'But I also see two things attacking her, which could so spoil her life that it's bright promise could be unfulfilled.'

'And what's wrong with me?' I shouted.

I could hear him and Mum laughing in the sitting room. I was wild.

'Oh,' I said, 'Elizabeth is wonderful and I am nothing.'

When he emerged from Mum's room, I said 'and what's wrong with me?'

'I will let you know Marjorie,' he said, and sure enough, a day or two later, he handed me a letter.

'You could be a most delightful person,' he said, 'but the two things attacking you are: one, your quick temper, and two, your love of showing off, so that people will think you plucky. But,' he added, 'what I admire in you is that if you are punished or chastised for something you have not done, then you will take your punishment and will not say that it was not you, or tell of the person who it was. I have great regard for you and know that you will go far.'

This placated me a little for I knew he was right, they certainly were my faults, and I marvel at how far-seeing he was, remembering that I was only one of two hundred girls.

One night he saw me and another girl apple scrumping. The next morning, his wife came into the kitchen where I was working to ask me if I would meet Uncle Ted at the apple trees at seven o'clock that evening, as he thought it best to clear the apples off before they all disappeared. Mrs Cooke added, 'They are such little monkeys to be scrumping, aren't they Marjorie?'

'Yes,' I replied, very seriously.

Prompt at seven o'clock he was there. Another girl and I went up into the trees.

'Careful!' he called.

'That's alright,' I said, 'the branch is quite safe, or at least it was the other night!'

We finished gathering the apples, which by the way were 'cookers'. Uncle Ted never told on us.

One further incident stands out in my mind. On Sunday evenings we had our own evening service, with various people coming to speak. My favourite was, of course, Mr Cooke. This particular Sunday, he was coming and I had misbehaved. Mother told me that I would be stopped from going to the service. Well after pleadings, I went, but Oh dear me, Uncle Ted's subject was about 'faces' and how he could read them and tell what sort of a face it was. He could tell whether they were happy or miserable, or whether they had been naughty. I felt myself becoming very uneasy and at the end of the service, when we filed out to go home, he stood at the door saying goodnight to each of us. I put my hands over my face and rushed past him. The next day he came to Rosebud and asked Mother what the problem was. Again I heard the chuckles!

Yes, we all loved him. He was a wonderful human being and I will be referring to him later in the book, as he became a father figure to me, and a steady influence in my life.

~ PART TWO ~

OUT
OF
THE
FOLD

11

On Monday 14th April I boarded the nine o'clock train from Clacton to Liverpool Street station in London, and from there, on to Alperton, Wembley, Middlesex. Mother, Miss Booth, had not yet returned from her sick leave, so I left without seeing her to say goodbye. That almost broke my heart.

The Sunday before I left, I went to our evening service and at the end they all sang 'God Be With You Till We Meet Again.' This hymn was always sung whenever one of the girls was leaving, and I remember when we used to sing it, feeling a little fearful of what may lay ahead for that person. Now, I felt that old fear, but this time it was for myself.

I arrived at Liverpool Street station feeling quite nervous, but before I reached the ticket barrier I saw Uncle Tom Hobbs. I cannot recall much of the journey to Alperton, Wembley. I only recall that when I arrived at the house, number 47, Stanley Park Drive, and went inside, I thought how small it was. We waited for dinner until my brother Harry came home from work. He worked shifts from 7.00 a.m. to 3.00 p.m.; then 3.00 p.m. to 11.00 p.m.; and then 11.00 p.m. to 7.00 a.m., as did Uncle Tom. They worked for the United Dairies (U.D.), Harry as an engineer and Uncle on the transport section. Fortunately, Harry was on the early shift on the day of my arrival.

While we waited for Harry, my aunt took me to see her sister Dorothy Woods, who was married to Uncle Jack Woods, a lovely man. I thought of him as 'a Cockney with a heart of gold.' He was a tram driver, based at the Stonebridge Park depot. They lived at Woodstock Road, Alperton, just a few doors from Georgie Woods, the actor and comedian (but no relation). As soon as they saw me they immediately said, 'Isn't she like Rene!'. When we got back to the house, I asked my aunt who Rene was. She seemed to evade the question, but when I went up to my bedroom, which was beautifully clean and had been especially prepared for me with my own wardrobe (what luxury!), Aunt and Uncle came into my room and said that they had something to tell me.

They started by saying that Mr Cooke did not think that I should be told immediately, for he felt that the shock would be too much for me, but because of the comments that they thought would be continually made about me looking like Rene, they had decided to have a talk with me.

Aunt Beatrice started by saying that the person called Rene was my eldest sister, Irene, who was married to Bill Darvill, lived at Neasdon and had a baby girl named Yvonne. Besides Rene, I learnt that I had a sister called Ivy, and another called Mabel, who was married to Ralph Willis. I also discovered that I had a twin brother and sister, Bill and Dorothy. Dorothy was married to Bert Sanderson. I could barely believe it all, but the biggest bombshell had yet to drop. They then said they were sorry to have to tell me that my father was still alive, that he had remarried, and there was also my stepmother Grace and stepsister and stepbrother, Eva and George.

After that I just felt devastated. Why had not my father bothered to write to me at Groom's? I understood that when Winifred had died he was informed and invited to Groom's to attend the funeral at Clacton, but nothing had been heard of him.

Never-the-less Aunt Beatrice and Uncle Tom said they were pleased to have me. Although they said that, in view of all that had been told me that evening, I felt completely unwanted. To think that I had been in John Groom's for fifteen years and apart from that chance meeting with Auntie May and Uncle Will Quinton, and then subsequently a visit from Aunt Beatrice, Uncle Tom, my cousin Roy, my brother Harry and his fiancée Doris, no-one, not even my father had bothered about me. Harry was only seven when our mother died. He left our father's house on the day he was eighteen (in fact as soon as he could), never to return.

In the next few days I was taken to see my mother's other sisters: an Aunt Grace Bletso who had a daughter Irene and a son Arthur; then another sister of my mother's called Flo who had a daughter Maisie. Aunt Flo was a lovely person but I thought her rather timid. She died in 1940. My mother also had a brother William, and his wife was called Flo. They had two daughters and a son. I was then taken over to Baker Street, Harlesdon, where Auntie May and Uncle Will Quinton lived, and there met their two daughters Madge and Joyce. My mother's brother Will Stephens was a train driver. One Sunday when I was walking with Aunt Beatrice we met them on their way home from Church. Evidently my Uncle Will was a very religious man. He had built a little mission church in Stonebridge park, just opposite a pub, and he used to preach there each Sunday. (My father also worked on the railway. He was the foreman of the maintenance men at Euston Station). What little I saw of uncle Will Stephens, I liked, but apart from meeting him again at Aunt Flo's funeral, I never saw him again.

I had been at Alperton about two weeks when Uncle Tom came home and said that he had arranged for me to have an interview at United Dairies (U.D.) head office. Everything was so new and confusing, I could not say where the head office was. I only know that I had to walk a fair way to catch a trolley bus. I was just walking along the North Circular road with Uncle Tom, going under what we called the Seven Arches, when disaster struck! Going for such an important interview I had naturally put my best clothes on, including a new pair of knickers. Suddenly my knicker elastic broke at the waist. What was I to do? I just stood and yelled 'Uncle!'. He tried to whistle a trolley bus, hoping that the driver would be Uncle Jack, but no, I had to walk from Stonebridge Park to Harlesdon to Auntie May's, all the while trying to hold up my knickers. We reached Auntie May's only to discover that she had no elastic, but she did find a piece of string. I tied this round my waist, caught a bus and arrived at my destination in time for the interview. The lady I spoke to was very kind and told me that she would try to find a position for me at the central offices at Western Avenue, Park Royal.

A few days later I went with my Aunt Beatrice to the U.D. offices at Park Royal and was interviewed by a Mr Whitehorn who was a thickset, stocky man, with white overalls on. I was absolutely petrified and when he asked me what the price of a dozen eggs would be at 'tuppence ha'penny' I could not for the life of me answer 'two and sixpence'. I was absolutely tongue-tied, fearing I would do or say the wrong thing. It was with fear and trepidation that I awaited his verdict, but yes, he said that he would give me a position in the addressograph room. I was told to report to him on the following Monday, and so on the 28th April 1938 I started work at United Dairies, Park Royal.

I was taken to a big room and introduced to the Head of the Department, a Miss Ness. She was a quiet, efficient person whom I got to like very much. The room was a big one, with about six addressal and four addressograph machines. In the front of the office sat two typists whose job it was to type the addressal cards and to keep the filing cabinets in order. At the back of the room was the graphotype machine, which was used to type the steel plates for the addressograph. The whole keyboard was in one long strip, the length of the graphotype. It had a big wheel at the front. You put the plate into a slot, moved the pointer to the figure or letter required, pulled a handle at the front of the keyboard and it printed the item selected. We had one lady who worked on the graphotype machine, which was quite a skilled job. We called her 'Knocky' because, I think, her name was Knox. She was a formidable but pleasant person, who showed great kindness to me. Although I, in common with everyone else, had 3d (three pence) stopped out of my wages for the 'Union Dues,' I had no idea what it all meant. I came to realise that Knocky was a very strong Trade Unionist, whatever that meant.

My wages started at fifteen shillings a week, so I received fourteen shillings and nine pence, which apart from two shillings and six pence, I had to give to my aunt. Out of the two shillings and six pence I had to keep myself in stockings and most Saturday afternoons I used to go to Woolworths in Wembley High Street, to buy them. They were nine pence a pair.

Well, back to the addressal machine. This had a wide desk-like top in front of it, and on the right hand side was a cage in which the square cards were placed. You pressed the pedals under the machine with your foot and the cards were then passed through to the inking roller, which came down and printed the customers' names and addresses on the invoices, books and ledgers for the roundsmen. The cards then dropped into a cage on the left hand side of the machine, which was of course placed low down. Round the office walls were the filing cabinets, which housed the trays of cards for the addressal machine, and then the smaller cabinets which housed the addressograph plates. On the front of the trays were the names of the depots, which covered practically the whole of the country. The United Dairies was indeed a very big firm. I remember that some of the depots had thousands of customers but there were also the smaller ones. For the addressograph there were only two depots printed on the plates, and each took a week to complete with the full list of all customers on the bills, books and ledgers. One lady was responsible for those two depots: Queenie Mansfield. She and Knocky were great friends. They were both looked up to in the office.

To start training on the machines we were given the job of printing just the lists. When you had reached almost the screaming point of boredom, Miss Ness transferred you on to printing the bills for the roundsmen. This was a different kettle of fish altogether. As the cards moved along the machine and were printed you had to remove each one. We had to have a fingerette on our index finger to enable us to get a firm grip on each bill and quickly remove it. We all of us felt at one time, whilst learning the job, that we would never be quick enough to master it. We would almost come to desperation point and then suddenly we managed it and we never looked back! We would print thousands each day. I remember one of the girls coming to help me out (we were given the smallest depots to start with), so that I could get my depot finished in time for despatch; and I remember doing the same myself on a couple of occasions for a new girl. Miss Ness came to me and said, 'Don't do too much for her or she'll never learn.' This was right for you just had to stick it out - just like learning to type really.

Each Friday afternoon we were given a worksheet for the following week, each worked out in days. The work had to be finished on the day stipulated for many items had to be despatched that day, out to the depots for the weekend collections and deliveries by the roundsmen. The U.D. did not only deliver milk, but all manner of groceries and tinned milk too. If a person was given a job at the U.D. and their parents were not customers, they would receive a hamper of groceries to encourage them to transfer their allegiance to the U.D. and it goes without saying that it invariably worked! On Friday lunchtimes we were allowed to go down to the stores to purchase certain items cheaply. They used to say that we could get cracked eggs and dented tinned fruit, soups and other commodities. But the eggs were rarely cracked or the tins dented. We could also buy bottles of various sauces, tins of meat, salmon and eggs that had cracked. It was a very good firm to work for in the main.

She did not spy on me again. I was very happy at work and made a few friends. There came a time when Queenie was away ill for two weeks. Miss Ness came and asked me to do her job, saying 'Don't worry if you get behind. See how it goes and if necessary I'll get one of the other girls to help you out. I felt quite exhilarated at being asked to do Queenie's job at the addressograph, and in all truth I did just as Miss Ness had instructed me, not rushing the job and just taking it steady. I was completely surprised when I found myself finishing it almost a whole day early. Then I went over the whole of the checking with her. Those big jobs had to be checked before going to the depots; in fact all books and ledgers had to be checked every day. Anyway, Miss Ness was very pleased with me, but not Knocky, or Queenie when she returned! I was lucky, possibly, that there were no hiccups such as the machine jamming.

As I have said, I made friends with the girls at work, two or three of my own age, and some older. There was Margaret from Perivale, who I remember spending a Christmas evening and Boxing Day with, staying overnight at her house. In fact it was so nice I was loathe to return to Alperton. We also at the beginning of the war, joined the Red Cross together, and I used to go over to Perivale on a Sunday morning for First Aid lessons. The instructor asked me if I had done it before as I seemed quite proficient at it. I said no, but secretly I thought of the common sense training I had received at John Groom's.

Another friend Marie, lived at Willesden. Margaret and I went with her to her local youth club, me for the table tennis. In summertime we were also allowed on the tennis courts, which was good fun. One evening at Perivale, the Red Cross put on a dance. I happened to see my sister Ivy's brother-in-law and asked him if he would like to go, but he said he would not be able to make it. So I set off alone, (a bit scared for I was afraid of the dark), but I got there all right and found Margaret waiting for me in the foyer. I told her that Bobbie was unable to come. 'Well never mind,' she said, 'there's a few young boys here to dance with.' So we settled down to a good evening. Margaret had a boyfriend who was in the Army, an Irish fellow. I remember I was dancing with someone when suddenly the lights went out. We thought it was an air raid. I felt someone get hold of my hand and then the lights clicked on. It was Bobbie! I had a crush on him at the time, so I was pleased, knowing also that I would not have to walk back to Alperton on my own in the dark. Don't ask me about the rest of the dance, but I am sure I enjoyed it.

A special friend of mine at the U.D. was Joan Parrot. Joan lived at South Harrow. We remained friends even after the war, but eventually lost touch. I have often wondered about her. We used to go out together most weekends and I used to stay at her house quite a lot. I remember one Saturday night in 1940, going to the King's Theatre, Hammersmith, to see Suzette Tary, and in the evening coming home in a raid and having to dodge into the street air-raid shelter. It was raining cats and dogs! In the afternoon we had shopped in Hammersmith, and I had bought a lilac crepe-de-chine dress. It had been too long for me so I had left it there to be shortened. I was to call back for it half an hour later. When I went back and tried it on, it had certainly been shortened! Nevertheless I couldn't do any other than accept it. I put it on to go to the theatre and as I have said it was raining heavily. By the time we had got to Joan's the wretched dress was almost up to my waist! We laughed ourselves silly. We certainly had many happy times together.

The United Dairies had a very good sports club and one day I was asked to go for a netball practise after work. This resulted in me being picked for their netball team. My cousin Joyce Quinton was also selected. She worked at Park Royal in the Burroughs and Comptometer room, but I had very little to do with her. I do not think that she wanted people to know I was related to her, knowing that I had been in an orphanage. However I remember one day, when I arrived home from work, my Aunt Beat went berserk at me, calling me a 'bloody little snob,' and 'A real bloody Todd.' She then boxed my ears. I asked what I had done but she just imitated my speech and said who did I think I was talking like that. She said that Joyce had told her that as she passed through our office on her way down to the stores one Friday, I had completely ignored her. Of this, I was totally unaware. I recalled that when I got into a temper over something at Groom's and lashed out, Mum stood her ground and said to me to 'Go on, hit me.' Of course that stopped me in my tracks. That incident actually came into my mind when Aunt Beat was boxing my ears and hitting me all over the place, and although I wanted to retaliate, I never did. Neither did I tell Harry.

Another sports club I joined was the table tennis club. How

I loved that game and used to play it in my dinner hour, for the UD had a table set up in their huge dining-cum-recreation room. Later on, the UD had their sports day covering the Eastern Area. I was chosen to go as a substitute runner for the Park Royal club. We went one mid-week afternoon over to Romford where the UD had a big sports ground. The weather was ideal and although I did not run that day I had a lovely time. It was certainly a new experience for me.

I used to go over to my friend Joan's house at South Harrow quite a lot and also to Ivy's (one of the typists who became a good friend to me). Her mum was a lovely homely person. She live on Ducane Road, Shepherds Bush, and her house backed on to Wormwood Scrubs Prison. The Saturday afternoon when the London Docks were heavily bombed, I well remember standing with Ivy on the Scrubs (a piece of wasteland by the prison) and watching the Docks burn. The sky was completely red and one could almost feel the heat of the fires. Opposite Ivy's house was a school. In the playground was a large Ack-Ack gun which would be fired during an air-raid. It was all for a psychological purpose, for everybody knew that there was no chance of it ever hitting the Jerry planes. That was the year of 1940. Indeed, for the Londoner, it was a year to remember for the war had started in real earnest with heavy air-raids every night.

12

A few months after going to live with Aunt Beat in 1938, I was out shopping with her one Saturday afternoon in Wembley High Street, when she said that she wanted to call in at the Butchers Shop, 'Walton, Hassel & Port'. A young man came up to my aunt and she said to him, 'Are you the person that is going to marry my niece Ivy Todd?' He acknowledged the fact and she said, 'Well, this is Ivy's youngest sister Marjorie, and she is living with me.' He was taken aback and said that Ivy would be seeing her soon. We came out of the shop and I saw a very smart young lady crossing the road and going towards the shop. I remember how very sophisticated she looked, with her high heels (which were all the fashion then) and her hair immaculate, with curls at the back of her head. She looked so full of confidence. Yes, it was my sister Ivy, whom I had never seen before! She was getting married at the beginning of August 1938 and we were immediately invited to the wedding, which was on a Sunday (It had to be on a Sunday as shops were open until 9 p.m. on a Saturday and closed for just half a day on a Thursday).

I remember the wedding well, for it was the first wedding I had ever been to, but more importantly, it was where I met the rest of my family. There was Rene, her husband Bill, and daughter Yvonne; May and her husband Ralph; Dorothy and her husband Bert; and Dorothy's twin brother Bill. It was quite an experience to suddenly meet all the family. What struck me was what a happy, uninhibited set of people they were, and I longed to get closer to them. My father was not there, and neither were my stepmother, George or Eva. In fact I have only seen them twice in my life.

Ivy's husband Bert had a younger brother called Bobbie, who was sixteen at the time. I was just fifteen and we became friends. We went to the pictures, and for walks together, and one Sunday in 1939 just at the beginning of the war he asked me if I would like to go to a show at Park Royal. Being brought up at John Groom's as I was it seemed quite an unforgivable thing to do on a Sunday, but Bobbie explained that it was a variety show and 'talent' night, and that Leslie Hutchinson (universally known as Hutch) was singing. Of course I succumbed and I shall never forget it. It was the first time I had been anywhere like it. I enjoyed seeing the famous singer 'Hutch' but what stays in my mind are the rows of young soldiers sitting in front of us. One of their pals got up to sing amidst his mates' catcalls. He was a good singer. Another soldier sat at the piano playing and singing 'Where or When.' A few weeks later we heard that they had all been killed in France. That was when the meaning of the war really came home to us, for one of the officers had worked in the office at the United Dairies. His mother was devastated, but this was just the beginning; millions of mothers were to go through the same trauma. It was indeed tragic and frightening.

In the early summer of 1939, Aunt Beatrice, Uncle Tom and my cousin Roy went on a holiday to Hastings, and I was invited to stay with Aunty Dorothy and Uncle Jack Woods. They had no children of their own. They lived very near to us, and Auntie Dorothy was often a visitor to our house, especially when Uncle Jack was on late turn. As stated before, Uncle Jack worked for the London Tram buses. They were well unionised and also had a good sports ground, with tennis courts, etc. which Uncle

Jack and Auntie Dorothy went to regularly in the summer, on Uncle Jack's rest days. It happened that in the week I went to stay with them, Uncle Jack had a Sunday rest day, so quite early that Sunday morning we set off for the sports club. What an enjoyable day it was! We had Sunday lunch there; I played tennis practically all afternoon; we had tea; and then in the evening there was dancing.   I went there a few times with Uncle Jack and Auntie Dorothy. Uncle Jack had a great liking for budgerigars and canaries. He had a big aviary in his garden and he would take me round showing the different birds to me.

At the end of the week with them, I was due, on the Saturday, to start my holiday. Where? Why, to John Groom's at Clacton-on-Sea! I was so excited. Uncle Jack and Auntie Dorothy came to Liverpool Street Station to see me off. I remember it as if it were yesterday, for the day was sunny and I was so impatient to get onto the train. You see, when we left John Groom's we were told that if we wanted a holiday at the seaside, we would be allowed to have a week on the same terms as everyone else, at the Holiday Home. I had written to Mr Cooke (Uncle Ted) to see if it was possible for me to go, and back came the reply that indeed I could. Matron Langridge then wrote to tell me that a room had been reserved for me at the Holiday Home.

As the train drew into Clacton, passing the recreation ground, I recalled how we had loved to wave to the passengers as the trains slowed down to go into the station. Now everything was reversed. I was one of the visitors. When I arrived at the station and was handing my ticket to the ticket collector, I saw two girls from Groom's. One was Marjorie Smith who I had once had to look after when little. Now she was a house-girl. They carried my case for me, chatting all the time. I remembered that one year when one of our 'old girls' had come back for a holiday at Groom's, it had been remarked that she now spoke quite posh. Well, I felt that I must also make an impression and put on my best voice, but being me, I could not keep it up!

Such a happy week it was. On Tuesday, the fete day, I enjoyed myself helping with the teas and selling the ice-creams, but when watching the fire display, how I longed to join in. Matron Langridge had set up different meetings and events in the afternoons, for the house-girls, and that Thursday afternoon was going to be a special event with prizes for the girls. She asked me to go into the town to get one or two things for her, and then invited me to the afternoon's meeting. Each girl was given her prize. Matron Langridge had asked me earlier which out of two prizes I thought would be most useful and I had told her. I did not expect, at the end of the meeting, also to be given a 'Prize', a manicure set I had unwittingly chosen myself. That was Matron Langridge all over.

I had very little money when I went on holiday, although I had tried to save up hard for it. What should I buy my aunt and Roy? I had spent very little so far, knowing I had to take them home something. Everything seemed so dear in the shops, so one evening I ventured into an Auctioneers', in those days like an open market. I stood and watched people buying things, mostly surprise packets, but they seemed quite pleased with their purchases. Eventually, after selling a few more 'wanted gifts' the time came again for a few more surprise packets at sixpence and nine pence. I bought one of each. The sixpenny one for Roy was a pen, and the nine penny one, for Aunt and Uncle, was a pretty plate to hang on the wall, which I thought quite nice. Not so the receivers! I have never indulged in that way of buying a present again.

Within a few weeks of returning from my holiday in Clacton, on Sunday 3rd September 1939, war with Germany was declared. I remember all of us just standing in the living room listening to Neville Chamberlain speaking on the radio at three minutes past eleven. He said that an ultimatum had been sent to Hitler demanding that he should withdraw his troops from Poland. Hitler had been told that he had until 11 a.m. to reply, saying that he would withdraw the troops. Otherwise we would declare war on Germany. No such reassurance had been received. I remember feeling bemused and also having a cold fear inside me.

Uncle Tom had served in the First World War and had on occasions told us things that had happened then (which I had always thought were not quite true). Now he said that he would like to 'have a go at the buggers again.' Seeing that he was over fifty and in a responsible job, I did not think that it was likely he would get a chance, or that he meant what he said. My brother Harry was twenty-four and expecting to be called up.

Early one Saturday morning in October, when I went down to breakfast, there was just Harry at the table. He had come off night work and everyone else was still in bed. He told me he was leaving Aunt Beatrice's and that he was intending to get married to Doris shortly, but he assured me that I would be all right staying with the Hobbs. I recall it as if it were yesterday, the awful sinking feeling as if my inside had turned over. But what could I say? That I would be scared to remain there without him? There was a war just commencing and he wanted to get married and set up home for himself and Doris. I kissed him and hoped that he would be very happy.

13

How empty it seemed when I returned from work and realised there would be no Harry. The beginning of the war was a very quiet affair at first. We heard that my brother Bill (who I had only seen once) was already in France on the 'Maginot Line.' I was shocked when my aunt said that it would be a good thing for Harry to go, and although she did not want him to be killed or any REAL harm to come to him, she thought it would do him good if he were injured a little. I felt furious with her. Harry and Doris did get married but we did not go to the wedding! A few months later Harry received his call-up papers. He joined the Royal Engineers, as he was an engineer at the U.D.

The United Dairies promised all staff who were called up that they would have their jobs waiting for them when they returned to Civvy Street. After the war they kept their promise, although of course, some did not return. What a waste of lives war is. Unlike the First World War however, this was not futile. It was a great evil we were fighting, although I (and many of my age and older) did not realise it then.

Harry was soon posted overseas to Syria in the Middle East. He was in Syria for almost six years, and strange to relate, he suffered a few weeks of snow blindness. Seems impossible, doesn't it! My friend Bobbie remained in Civvy Street, but he worked as a fireman on the railways. I remember one evening when Bobbie came round to see me we were sitting at the table in the living room when an air raid started. Suddenly there was a loud 'crump' and all the lights went out. My aunt stood in between the living room door and passage in a nervous state, as were we all. Uncle Tom Hobbs was walking up and down telling us not to panic (like the character Corporal Jones in Dad's Army) and saying to calm us 'The Buggers won't get away with it!' He'd defeated them before!

The bomb had fallen at the back of our house, which backed onto the Wembley High School playing field. Bobbie and I had sat at the table just holding hands, to give each other a bit of courage. The lights came on quite soon afterwards and then suddenly my aunt shouted 'Look at her! There she sits all calm. The bloody Todd.' I was as afraid as anyone, but what could I do? The other girls who I worked with at the U.D. had decided when a daytime raid occurred that the only way to cope with it was to say to yourself that no matter what you did, if your name was on it (meaning a bomb) you would just get it. It was the only attitude to take. I was sixteen at the time.

We used to go down to the air raid shelter in the garden, with a flask of tea laced with rum, but it became so very damp and cold. Eventually brick shelters were erected, part on the road and part on the pavement, and as the air raids in 1940 became heavier we went in them. At least my aunt, uncle Tom and Roy did, and I on a couple of occasions. As the raids grew particularly heavy over Willesden way (for the raiders were evidently after the railway junction) my other aunts and their families came over too. At first we all tried to squeeze in, and I distinctly remember one night having to sleep with my head out of the shelter; hence a very stiff neck in the morning. I was then told that there was no room for me so I just slept in my own bedroom in the house. One night another bomb fell very close to the house and my uncle came into the house calling 'Are you all right?' I felt like not answering him.

Things became very, very tricky for me living there, and one evening I spoke to Bobbie about it. He told me to have a word with Aunt Beat about it. I did. She went berserk and I saw that it was impossible for me to remain there. I told Bobbie the outcome and the next night when he called for me he said he was going to see his brother and my sister. They had not been married very long but Bert was due to go in the R.A.F. in a couple of weeks time, so he and my sister agreed that I should go to live with them at Wembley Hill. On the following Saturday afternoon I collected my things and (Thank God) left my aunt's house forever. What a relief it was!

It was at this same time, that I changed my job. Before I left the Hobbs' household my aunt thought that I should earn more money so she took me to an employment agency in Wembley High Street. There was a vacancy for an addressograph operator at the B.B. Biscuits firm. I think that it was in Scrubbs Lane. I applied for the job although the money was only four shillings more than I was earning at the U.D.

That Thursday I gave my week's notice to Mr Whitehorn and he said, 'That's a pity. I have had good reports of you and I was thinking of putting you on the Burroughs machines and then onto the comptometers.' I did not really believe him and thought that he was just saying this because I was leaving. However, the following Friday, when I received my pay packet, on the payslip there had been a twelve shilling rise (in those days very substantial) which had been crossed out. I was furious and went to Mr Whitehorn and demanded to see the director. With a smirk, that was granted, and when I went into his office I told him that it was a despicable and crooked thing to do; that there was a principle at stake. He in turn became angry at what he said was my effrontery, started to shout and told me to leave the room, adding 'I'll have a word with your father!' As in my opinion I had no father, I just left his office without a word.

A week later, with mixed feelings, I left the U.D. It was also the weekend that I left living at 47, Stanley Park Drive, Alperton, Wembley. During the week before I had heard that a man living a few doors away from us had evacuated his wife and child to the country, as he was soon due to be called up. He was a musician and playing in a popular band at the time, which because of the call-ups and the fact that they were all young players, was thinking of disbanding. He was selling his house so he needed somewhere to live. The morning I left, Beatrice Hobbs said she had already agreed to let him have my room as a 'paying guest.'

Whilst living with my aunt I had an opportunity to go to a John Groom's reunion. I went over to Edgeware and Mr Cooke took me. At the reunion I met my friend from throughout my Groom's days, Phyllis Singleton, and I discovered that she was in service at Ealing. One Bank Holiday Monday when she was given some time off, I went over to meet her at Ealing Broadway, and from there we went to Kew Gardens which became a favourite place of mine. Having 'found' each other we decided to keep in touch and on a couple of occasions my aunt allowed me to invite Phyllis over to tea.

When I left Alperton I still owed my aunt some money for clothes and my sister suggested that I should pay it all off. So one Sunday afternoon I went once again to Stanley Park Drive to pay off my debt. When I arrived, to my surprise and consternation, I found Phyllis there sitting in a chair. I was unable to speak to her and years later, when I met up with Phyl again, she explained that she had had a most uncomfortable time there that day. She told me that Aunt Beat was a terrible person and that she had said all manner of untrue things about me. She never went there again and after that incident I cut off all ties with that side of the family. I wrote to Phyllis to tell her the reason why I left.

14

My new job with B.B. Biscuit firm was a disappointment. Their addressograph section turned out to be just a small space with two addressograph machines, staffed by just one young girl and a young man. I was stuck in a very small space at the end of a long office. Within a fortnight I left, for it was most unsatisfactory all-round. But having got the job through an employment agency, I still owed them a week's wages. I had to find something quick. My sister Ivy was working at that time in a war factory at the back of the Stadium, so I decided that perhaps I could try the same. I found a position at a metal factory, near Wembley High Street, and thought I would give it a try for I had to do something! I cannot say that I was very nimble at the job; I was bored to tears and hated the atmosphere of the place.

I was eventually shifted to the spraying shed and packing department. The metal plates were extremely hot coming off the belt and I recall a young woman there who had to pull big heavy loads of the plates into the main factory from the spraying shed. She was being ostracised because she was an unmarried woman expecting a baby. I learnt that her soldier boyfriend had been posted overseas before they could be married. She still heard from him, but in those hypocritical days things were made uncomfortable for girls who had 'sinned.' Young as I was (seventeen years old) I felt very, very sorry for her, and knowing just what often did go on I always felt that there were many in those days who could say to themselves 'There but for the grace of God go I.'

One day, the head of the factory approached me to see if I would like to do the metal workmen's worksheets, as the person so employed was away. I sat on a stool, on a sort of dais, in the factory metal works. As the men were given a job to do they brought their work sheet to me at the start and finish of the job, and I had to fill it in for them. This I felt, was more in my line. What was recorded on the worksheet related to the bonus that they would receive in their pay packet at the end of the week. I did this job for about a month and then the person returned, but the next time she was away I was asked to do the same.

One of the staff came down from the office, from where they worked out the men's bonuses, to collect the sheets. Once I was asked to take them to the main office, which I did. The sense of snobbishness I felt there was unbelievable! I, in their minds, was a factory hand. I do not know if today, there is still such a snobbish division, but what I do think is that these office workers failed to realise that if there were no factory workers, skilled or otherwise, there would be no need for office workers. They only had their jobs because of the production of factory workers; it was they who kept the business going. You need hand and brain, not just the one.

At the weekend we finished work, even in wartime, at one p.m. on Saturdays, and on occasions I would go over to Neasdon, to see my sister Irene and her baby Yvonne. Bill her husband, had been called up and was in the Army. I enjoyed going there for I liked Rene a lot.

After work on weekdays, I used to meet Ivy on my way home to Wembley Hill, where we lived. Just a few months previously I had started going to evening classes for shorthand and typewriting, but because of the air raids they had closed down. Ivy and I would go home together and because invariably there would be a raid on, for they started as soon as it was dusk, we would end up by going straight into our shelter. When the all clear went we would nip into the house to get our bedding (blankets and pillows), and also a little cooking stove to boil water or milk on. By that time, another air raid would have started again. We would have something to eat and drink and then it would be time to turn down and try to get some sleep. However, we would have to wait for the all-clear to go again before we could take the saucepan and stove back and really settle down for the night.

One night I said to Ivy, 'I'll take the equipment back.'

'Wait a minute,' she said, 'there is a plane up there.'

'Don't be silly,' I said. 'The all-clear has gone. That is one of ours.'

I was just going out of the doorway of the shelter when she suddenly grabbed me, pulled me to the ground and shoved a pillow over my head.

'What are you doing?' I shouted.

She had heard the bomb falling, straight onto the house where the shelter was, and if I had continued to go into the flat, I would most likely have been killed. Ivy had saved my life! The A.R.P. who were at the bottom of our road, came running up the street, for they thought that Ivy and I had 'caught it' and that it had been a direct hit on the shelter. Unfortunately, a chap in the house had stood outside watching this plane. Just a few days previously, he had sent his wife and children to be evacuated to the country. He had bought himself a new suit and was intending to go down that weekend to visit them. The poor man caught the blast and both his legs were trapped. While the A.R.P. men were releasing him and lifting him onto a stretcher, he said to them, 'I've got a new suit in the wardrobe to see the missus in. Look after it for me.' I never knew what became of him.

Most days, Ivy and I went to work in an air-raid, and came home in one. Such was the Blitzkrieg in 1940. One morning when we were walking to work, Ivy pulled me across the road and put her hands over my eyes, telling me to look straight ahead. The reason for this was that during an air-raid a gas main had been hit and they were putting the bodies on the paths.

On Saturday afternoons we used to go and do the shopping early, so as to get home before an air-raid started, treat ourselves to a fire and have our tea and crumpets indoors. Sheer luxury in those days! Well, this particular Saturday, we had gone to Harlesden to do some shopping. Ivy had finished hers, but I wanted some new shoes - silver sandals! The war could not last forever, I thought. The consequence was that I could not find any, but I did cause us to miss the trolley bus to Wembley Hill. Ivy was not very pleased about it. Every minute counted if we wanted to have our tea indoors before a raid. Well the next bus came. We got on it and got off, as always, at the Harrow tavern, our road being next to it. When we arrived at the tram stop, what did we see? The tram that we had missed had been strafed, by a lone enemy plane, although the sirens had not gone off.

This was a most hectic period of my life, but for all the dangers, I was at least happy living with Ivy; a hard-working and very caring sister indeed. I was treated as an equal - a person in my own right.

Shortly after these happenings, Ivy and I went to live with her in-laws at Alperton. A very few weeks later, Ivy heard from her sister-in-law (who lived at Vernon Avenue, Belmont, Stanmore), that a man who owned a house just a couple of streets away from hers, was looking for a tenant to rent it. 'Was Ivy interested?' Ivy contacted Rene, and a few weeks later, Rene with Yvonne (who was three), Ivy and I moved into 61, Hermitage Way, Belmont, Stanmore.

What a relief it was to go to bed normally, and to sleep once more in a real bed! For over six months, Ivy and I had had to 'sleep' in an air-raid shelter. Rene told me that the night she was 'bombed out,' she was sitting in the house with Yvonne on her knee and literally saw the walls of the house parting. I have always admired both my sisters Rene and Ivy. They were both very brave people. I very much liked the house at Hermitage Way, and I know that both Rene and Ivy's husbands were relieved that they were living in a safer area.

When we moved to Belmont in 1941 I knew that I must start to make a serious decision as to what my future must be. I worked for a little while at the G.C.E at North Wembley, doing shift work from 6 a.m. to 2 p.m. (or from 2 p.m. to 10 p.m.) I used to get up at 4 a.m. in order to have a good half an hour to do my hair. Trying to emulate the smartness of Ivy, I used to put at least fifty Dinkie curlers in my hair and diligently comb each one out separately, making my hair a mass of curls which was all the fashion then. I never had it 'permed', just occasionally set.

I remember while I was at the G.C.E. listening to a new programme that had started on the radio called Workers' Playtime. The comedians and singers went all over the country to different factories, to record their programmes. This caused much excitement among the workers, but myself, I was never fond of variety playhouses. You were not forced to go. All this was devised to keep the workers happy and morale high. In other words, a happy worker is a hard and efficient worker, and their high production was crucial to the war effort. The programmes also included propaganda to make us realise the evil we were fighting against.

When I finally decided to join the W.A.A.F. I changed my job once again, to save all the expense of travelling, and worked for about three months at Woolworths in Belmont Circle. On my eighteenth birthday, 8th March 1941, I sent my application form off to the Air Ministry, hoping that I would be accepted into the W.A.A.F. Within a fortnight I went for a medical and interview. On the 27th May I arrived home from work and Rene said to me, 'Your call-up papers have come.' I opened the envelope. I should have gone that very day! Looking at the postmark I noticed that it had previously been sent to Belmont in Surrey. It causes me amusement now, that I wrote off straight away to the Air Ministry, asking if they would 'reconsider my application' for their letter had gone to Belmont in Surrey instead of Belmont in Middlesex

A month later, I again received my call-up papers, instructing me to report to the Air Ministry on the 14th July 1941. From London I went with about a dozen other girls to start my training at Insworth Lane, Gloucester. So began a new phase of my life. I must mention that when I left Belmont, my sister Ivy walked to the gate with me and said that although I was going away, there would always be a home for me with her at Belmont. She was worried about what dangers I might be facing, but as it turned out, the civilian population were to experience far greater dangers than many of us.

15

We arrived at Insworth Lane at about 5 p.m. and after being given a hot meal we were directed to the different huts we were to sleep in. The next morning after breakfast we were given a 'pep' talk and then told of the day's procedures. First we had to visit the Medical Officer to receive vaccinations for various diseases, including tetanus. 'Swing your arms around,' they said after the injections. 'That will take the hurt away.' During the night I heard moaning and tears from some of the other beds. My own right arm ached; my left arm did not. The reason for this was that when received into John Groom's all children were immediately vaccinated against smallpox. The girls suffering in the W.A.A.F. had never been vaccinated.

We were told by the W.A.A.F. officer on our inception at Insworth lane, 'If you can stick the next couple of weeks you will be able to stick anything.'

Although our arms were very swollen and aching (we could barely lift them) we were nevertheless sent out on parade the next day to do physical training. Here 'physical jerks' would certainly be the most appropriate phrase, for in the exercises we could just not put our right arms up! I recall the physical training over those first two weeks with quite a sense of mirth, for we were all volunteers and such was the situation in the country that we had to do our training in our civilian clothes. As it was July, we must have been quite a sight touching our toes in our light, short summer frocks. It was only at the end of the first week that we were kitted out in our W.A.A.F. uniforms.

After the first ten days at Insworth Lane, we were all allowed a half-day trip to Gloucester. My first impression was of a dark and dingy place, dominated by a cathedral. Naturally our first trip was to a photographer's. They must have done a roaring trade. We were told to call back in an hour's time. This we did and on entering the shop noticed the wall at the back of the counter covered with new recruits' photographs. Waiting in turn to get ours, we were criticising these photographs. One, I said, looked like a miserable sergeant major. I handed my ticket in, and yes, the miserable sergeant major was me! There must be some mistake I thought, but on close inspection, yes I was the ugly bug.

We had two dress uniforms in air force blue, two skirts and two tunics. One was for every day and one was for best. We were given knickers of thick, dark material that we christened 'blackouts.' The heavy, air force blue greatcoats were very smart. There was not a greatcoat to fit me at that time, so I was given a lined, air force raincoat, which was really for officers only. It was not until a few months later that I eventually got a greatcoat.

We attended lectures and were given warnings, as we were young girls, not to let our heads be turned by the young men we would be working with on the air force stations. Although they would be in smart air force uniforms, we should not be taken in by them, but find out about their civilian circumstances.

At the end of our training, we were all called once more into the lecture room and told which air force stations we were to be sent to. One member of each group was to be put in charge, to be responsible for everyone during the travelling, and to give their credentials to the flight sergeant on arrival at the R.A.F. station. That person had to stand up when her name was called out, so that the other members of the group would know who she was. I was amazed when they called my name and I had to stand up as the one in charge of the group going to the R.A.F. Station at Oakington in Cambridgeshire. I thought that it must have been my double-barrelled name. There was a W.A.A.F. in our group called Mrs Thwaites who was to be an administration officer, who thought that she would obviously be put in charge. However, I stood up and was given the list of names and the information that was to be handed to the Flight Sergeant when we arrived at Oakington.

We went back to our huts to prepare for an equipment and hut inspection. We were also told to polish the floor by our beds and in the middle of the hut. I did the middle of the floor of the hut for us all. We were waiting for the inspection when Mrs Thwaites came into our hut to say that there must have been a mistake, that she should be in charge and that I should hand her the documents. 'No,' I said, 'I shall hand over the documents myself when we get to Oakington.'

Next morning, we were all taken to Gloucester Station. I did keep a watchful eye on Mrs Thwaites because I had never travelled far before and I thought that as she must be in her forties, she would know her way around. She had three or four girls with her, but I also had friends with me. Travel was so very slow in those days that we did not arrive at Cambridge station until about 5.30 p.m. Transport was already waiting for us. I duly handed over the documents, but I had a feeling that Mrs Thwaites had already spoken to the flight sergeant, who I noticed, seemed quite amused.

We were the first eleven W.A.A.F.s on Oakington station, apart from one W.A.A.F. who had preceded us by a couple of weeks. We were accommodated in the nearby village of Long Stanton, where two big houses had been requisitioned by the Air Ministry. One house, near Long Stanton Station was called Redlands. The other house, about half a mile away, in the village, was called Brookefields. Brookefields was a sort of headquarters, the place where we went for our meals, etc. The cooks were billeted there. I was billeted at Redlands, which I thought was a beautiful place with a lovely garden. There was a big lawn and at the bottom of the lawn was a row of poplar trees. But lovely as this house was, there was no running water. Each evening before going to bed, we would go into the kitchen-cum-scullery to pump up the water. There were so many pumps if you just wanted a wash, but many, many more if you wanted a bath, and generally every evening we bathed. We were quite happy, taking turns and helping each other, for it was a new experience to us all. We were not at Redlands for long because after a while, huts were built on camp to accommodate the W.A.A.F.s.

I liked the flight sergeant for she was a jolly person and had a keen sense of humour. She watched over us all like a mother, and one day she spoke to me because she was worried about me getting into the wrong company. There was a public house next door to our billet and one girl, older than I, suggested that we go there of an evening for a drink and a sing-song. It was not my way of spending an evening but I went, having nothing better to do, although I only drank a shandy. This I did for three nights running, but then the flight sergeant spoke to me and I never went there again.

My first job as a W.A.A.F at Oakington was in the Intelligence section, being a runner and taking messages. The shifts were from 7 a.m. to 3 p.m., 3 p.m. to 11 p.m., and 11 p.m. to 7 a.m. During the night shifts we would help the air crews prepare to set off on their bombing missions to Germany. What time they went depended upon the time of year and where they were going. After seeing them off, we often had a lull in activity while we waited for them to return. As soon as they arrived back we gave them cigarettes and coffee laced with rum, as they would be freezing cold from the raid, even though they did have fur-lined leather jackets and fur-lined flying boots. Having warmed up, the airmen went to be interrogated by intelligence officers who needed to know where their bombs had dropped and other details.

Of course many aircrews did not return. The average life expectancy of a crew was three months and we lost many of our friends. It was very hard to come to terms with. To cope we would be quite flippant, saying 'Oh, so-and-so's copped it now,' but in fact it was heart breaking.

Each bombing raid was called an 'op' (operation) and a 'tour' was thirty ops. One squadron leader, Hamish Mulhadie had a crew that seemed to be amazingly lucky. They were preparing for the last op of their third tour when Hamish Mulhadie was unwell and the doctor refused to let him fly because he had the flu. After this op, the crew were due for a rest. In fact, the next day they were going to Buckingham Palace to receive special awards. That night they all perished

I was sent for one morning and told to report to the head W.A.A.F. officer. It was with a certain amount of trepidation that I was shown into her office. She told me that each of our two squadrons at Oakington, Number 7 Squadron and Number 101 Squadron, required one of us to work in the office of the hangars, on general duties. I was told to report to the commanding officer of 101 Squadron. He was a very nice man and popular with the air crews. One fine morning he came into the office and asked me if I would like a little 'trip'. I literally jumped at the opportunity. He said he was just going over to Lossiemouth in Scotland.

At that time, in 1941, R.A.F. Oakington just had Blenheim and Wellington bombers, and our plane was to be a Wellington. The commanding officer opened a wardrobe to find me the 'smallest' flying suit and then I went with it into the crew room.

Many of the boys were sitting on tables and they were amused to see me start to don the flying suit. The suits had a zip that started in the middle of the back, zipped down through the legs and then up to the neck. My suit was far too big for me of course and I had to bunch the arms and legs up because they were much too long. I was given a packed parachute, which I held by the handle, having no idea what I would do if I needed it. The aircrew boys watching me asked if I wanted any sickness pills or barley sugars but I just 'pooh-poohed' the idea. Well, the closed-in truck came and I clambered into it with the lads.

The body of the Wellington had no individual seats, just a strip of canvas on the right-hand side. On the left was the chute down which flares were sent. In the middle were a couple of steps and a small loo. We took off. After a while, when the pilot had finished all his plotting and duties, he asked me if I would like to look through the nose of the plane. I was game for anything! It meant climbing over a small partition and lying flat on the floor. Yes, I found it 'interesting' but the engines were immediately under my body. I began to feel very sick and afraid to move. The pilot commented to the crew 'She's enjoying herself so much, she doesn't want to get up!' The fact was that I couldn't get up because I was feeling too sick. Then I was very sick.

We arrived back mid-afternoon and I could barely wait for the evening meal, as I was feeling so empty! Although I said nothing to anyone about this incident, a few days later it was decided that this was not the right sort of job for a W.A.A.F. Another W.A.A.F. was doing the same job for Number 7 Squadron and she was also removed.

I was then transferred to the Signals section as a runner, taking messages to different departments and areas of the aerodrome. The people in the Signals Section were a very snooty lot. Shortly after I began working with them we heard news that King George V1 was going to visit Oakington. They were all highly elated, but I was not, so during the visit I was kept out of the way and a few weeks later transferred to the Officers' Mess as a batwoman.

I was a batwoman for a while, cleaning the officers' rooms, pressing their uniforms and generally looking after them. One officer always played classical music on his violin before he went on an op and I loved standing outside his room to listen. The morning after we had suffered heavy losses and five aeroplanes had not returned from a mission, I was asked to help the administration officer clear the rooms of those who had been killed. I remember clearing the room of a young officer and seeing the photograph of his wife and small child on the bedside cabinet. It really brought the tragedy of war home to me.

I have always regretted missing meeting the father of another officer I looked after, who had become a prisoner of war. He had written to his father and mentioned that he had a very good batwoman. The father visited the camp and asked to see the batwoman, but unfortunately I was away on a training course and he mistakenly spoke to someone else instead. He gave her five pounds. Of course I was not too concerned about the money when my friends told me, but I should very much liked to have spoken to the young man's father.

One day during 1943 when I was on telephone duty, I was sitting in the foyer of the officer's mess during a slack period, writing a letter to my boyfriend, Ernest. Sitting in the foyer close by, was the writer H.E. Bates. He was at Oakington in order to go out on an op and get an authentic idea of the experience before writing his book called *A Moment In Time*.

'Are you writing to your young man?' he asked.

'Yes,' I replied.

'Write from the heart, my dear,' he said. 'Write from the heart.'

Part of being on telephone duty involved cleaning the foyer and on one occasion I was told to give the floor a thorough polish, as there was going to be an inspection by the commanding officer, who was due to leave the next day to work in a different area. So I polished the floor thoroughly. When the commanding officer came, he walked in and slid across the floor falling on to his back. They helped him up and he continued his inspection. That evening there was a camp dance and who should I see approaching me but the commanding officer! He asked for a dance and during our waltz he said, 'You did a good job today.' He was a man with a good sense of humour.

After being a batwoman, I applied to work in the camp Post Office and being accepted, was sent on a training course at the Post Office Head Sorting Office in Mount Pleasant, London. Here I was trained to sort one hundred letters in three minutes I also learnt to work at the counter. I was then able to become a Postal Clerk at Oakington. My colleague, Marion, who trained and worked with me, became a great friend. She and I have kept in touch and remained friends all our lives. Our first job was to collect the mail from Long Stanton railway station at 7 a.m. each day. Marion and I took it in turns to do this. The mail all had to be sorted by 11 a.m., in time to be collected by different sections around the camp. The airmen's mess always brought us a jug of hot, sweet tea when they came for their mail. Later in the day, Marion and I had to empty the mail from the post boxes around the camp and a driver would then deliver our mailbags to the main sorting office at Cambridge. On Sundays we had to go with a driver to Cambridge, to collect the in-coming mail.

There were of course, periods of 'leave'. We were all entitled to go on leave for seven days, twice a year. We also had forty-eight hours leave once every three months. Before going on leave we had to take a form to be signed by the medical officer and if we were not up to date with our vaccinations, we had to have them. When not on leave, we were allowed out in the evenings but had to be back on camp by 22.30 hours. We were allowed two late passes a week, which meant we could stay out until 23.59 hours. On Friday it was payday and my friend Joan and I often went into Cambridge. First, we would treat ourselves to a slap-up meal at a restaurant and then we would go to the Victoria cinema.

Whatever job one did as a W.A.A.F. at Oakington, everyone had to do a regular turn in the Guardroom, on guard duty. I was on guard duty on Wednesday 8th May, 1945 - V.E. night. We had all been given the day off after the parade that morning and I had chosen to bike over to see my fiancé Ernest's mother. I was not sure how she would be feeling at the end of the war in which her youngest son had died. When I returned I had to do guard duty as usual, but fortunately for me, most of the celebrations took place on the following night.

On the Thursday evening the big quadrangle in the middle of the barracks block became the central meeting point. Some of our aircrews had flown over to Germany during the day and I don't know how they managed it, but they came back with several swastika flags. These were put onto a bonfire in the middle of the quadrangle and burnt. Some people got very excited and wanting more fuel, ripped off wooden toilet seats to feed the flames. That evening was the first time that I ever tasted gin and I was a little merry when I got back to our hut. My friend Marion, a teetotaller, whose brother was a Minister of the Church was ashamed of me! On the next payday we all discovered that some of our wages had been stopped in order to pay for the restoration of the toilets.

~ PART THREE ~

INTO
A
SAFE
HARBOUR

16

When we first went to Oakington and were billeted in Long Stanton, we found that the people in the villages of both Long Stanton and Willingham were very friendly towards us W.A.A.F.s. They often invited us to their homes for supper and occasionally a colleague and I were invited to a house at Willingham. The husband was a market gardener and his wife, Brenda, was a lot younger than him. They had two children called David and Barbara, aged about six and three.

One evening when we were visiting them, we met Brenda's cousin who had popped over for supper. He was from a village called Bluntisham and his name was Ken Ward. A few of us had recently had our photographs taken and I had given one to Brenda. She gave it to Ken, who took it home and showed his brother Ernest, who was at home on leave from R.A.F. Chipping Warden, near Oxford. Ernest decided that he would cycle over to his cousin's house to see this W.A.A.F. if Brenda would let him know when I would be there.

So Ernest and I met for the first time. We sat and chatted by the fire and he offered me a cigarette. During the evening, as we talked, I noticed what kind blue eyes he had; what an open face; and most of all, what beautiful, gentle, expressive hands. At the end of the evening he walked with me to my billet at Redlands. He seemed to be rather a quiet, serious chap, but he did ask me if I would write to him, and I agreed, knowing full-well how welcome a letter is when you are away from home. So began our friendship.

A few months later Ernest wrote to say that he was going home on leave and hoped to see me again. I had already put my forty-eight-hour pass in, to go home, and wrote to tell him so, saying that I would be sorry to miss him but that my home came first. However, when I returned from my leave, I discovered that Ernest was on ten days embarkation leave and that he wanted to see me. I met Ernest a few times at his cousin's house whilst he was home on leave, and each time he walked me back to Redlands. At the end of his leave I promised to continue to write to him, probably a bit more often.

Ernest left England on the 14th April 1942, for the Middle East. As soon as he was able, he wrote to me giving his new address, and I replied quickly, for it was an address en-route to his final destination with the Persia and Iraq forces. Strangely enough, my letter turned out to be the first letter he received after landing at his destination. It took three months to get to him. So began our courtship by post. Although I had agreed to write to him, I thought he was too quiet and serious a person for me. However, we discussed many, many things in our letters and found that our basic attitudes and beliefs were very much the same. The letters came almost daily, sometimes each of us receiving three or four at a time. In spite of the fact that he was on a wartime posting abroad, Ernest was able to appreciate the opportunity to travel for the first time in his life, and above all to visit the Biblical places such as Nazareth, Jerusalem and Bethlehem, where he had the chance to see the grotto of the Nativity. His letters also described a trip to Ur of Chaldees, the birthplace of Abraham, and the thrill he felt 'to walk along the roads once trodden by Abraham, and to enter the ruins of houses where he may have visited or even lived.'

At that period one way of sending a short letter was by Airgraph. An Airgraph was written on just one sheet of paper, and then the message from the page was photographed to make it a quarter of the size. This reduced the bulk of so many letters being sent long distances by Airmail. There was also an Airmail Letter Card, which you could get more writing on. This was made of flimsy paper, geared to reduce weight. Our main correspondence was by letter, for which you could get special airmail writing pads. A parcel could take up to as much as three months (sometimes even six) to reach its destination - if it was not lost at sea! Such was the precariousness of the war situation. Many people through 'Players' sent packets of 100 cigarettes to reach their men-folk. Of course each parcel was eagerly received although some arrived too sodden to be of any use. On several occasions I sent Ernest a Players parcel of cigarettes. We were not aware in those days of the harm that tobacco smoking could do to one's health.

There was not much in the shops. Virtually everything was rationed so parcels to your loved ones consisted mainly of razor blades, shaving cream and after shave lotion - the latter being needed because of the intense heat drying up the skin. Chocolate had to be saved up from one's meagre ration of four ounces a week. I also used to send the latest song sheets, which were mostly printed on a page of The News Of The World each Sunday, and which were eagerly seized upon by the troops abroad.

On the 8th October 1943 I received an Air Letter from Ernest asking me if I would consider marrying him, although it might be several years before he returned to England. It was way back in 1942 when I had suddenly realised (although I had been friendly with other chaps on the R.A.F. station) that it was definitely Ernest I would want for a husband. I remember that day distinctly. I vowed to myself then that I would never go out with any of the chaps on camp again, and that I would remain faithful to Ernest. When I received his letter on the 8th October I was overjoyed at the fact that he wanted to marry me.

I answered Ernest's letter straight away and agreed to wait for him even though it may be several years. I was surprised and exhilarated when suddenly on the 28th February 1944 I received a letter from him telling me that he had landed in England, at Liverpool, on the 26th February and would be coming home on disembarkation leave on the 28th.

Because I was engaged to Ernest I was granted seven days leave when he returned from abroad. We met for the first time after his return at the house of some friends called the Christmas's, in Willingham. After not having seen him for almost two years I did feel rather shy.

For Ernest it was a difficult time of adjusting to life back in England, and also for coming to terms with the loss of his beloved younger brother Ken, with whom he had been so close throughout the whole of their childhood. When Ernest had left home to go abroad, Ken had still been a civilian. In the interim period he had become a Flight Engineer in the R.A.F. His plane was shot down and he and the pilot had died (being the last to have to leave the aircraft), although the rest of the crew had survived to become prisoners of war.

We took this period of getting to know each other again slowly. On the Wednesday after Ernest's return we went to Cambridge and watched the film 'Sweet Rosie O'Grady, starring Bette Davies. At the weekend I went to Bluntisham, to stay at Ernest's parents' house and it was there that I celebrated my 21st birthday the following week. Ernest's mother and father were kindness itself to me. On my 21st birthday his mother lent me a beautiful pearl necklace to wear with a pretty dress that Marion, my colleague and W.A.A.F. friend had lent me for the occasion.

After his disembarkation leave Ernest returned to Morecambe Dispatch Centre, but in a few days he was posted to R.A.F. Little Staughton, near St. Neots, Huntingdon. This was a wonderful posting, just twenty-five miles from home, and it gave us a chance to really get to know each other. Ernest took his bicycle to the R.A.F. station with him, so that he would be able to cycle those few miles home on his days off. He asked me to get my twenty-four hour passes at the same time as his whenever possible, and this I agreed to do. We met many times, not only on twenty-four hour passes. We would both cycle halfway and meet at Huntingdon; or we would meet at the thicket, a beauty spot at St. Ives. We had our own little gate there where we would meet and sometimes say goodbye.

This delightful situation lasted for three months. Then with the 'buzz bombs' reigning down on London, Ernest's regiment was posted to Sheerness on the Kent coast, to try and shoot them down over the sea and prevent them getting through to London. (Buzz Bombs were so named by the people of Britain because their un-piloted engines could be heard droning overhead. When suddenly the engine cut out, the plane would fall and whole streets would be devastated).

At the beginning of June 1944 all leave was cancelled, but we were allowed a thirty-six hour pass once a month. June 6th 1944 was the beginning of the invasion of Europe. My own brother Bill was one of the first to land in France on that day. He told me that they all felt very groggy, waiting in a very choppy sea before the landings took place. Now, at last, it was England's turn to invade. Churchill's team, supported by the brave secret agents (one name that immediately springs to mind is that of the woman agent, Sybil Butler) had laid the plans well, and our great Field-Marshall Bernard Montgomery, affectionately called

'Monty' by the troops, put them into action. Monty was revered and respected by all of the troops who had great faith in his leadership and ability. He was a small man in stature but to the troops he was a giant in heart and deed. My brother told me that they would follow him to the ends of the earth, such was their faith in him.

Anyway, thirty-six hour passes were better than nothing and as Ernest could travel easily by train to London, we decided that I should get a thirty-six hour pass and travel from Cambridge to my home, even if it meant, as it invariably did, having just one evening together. Ernest immediately liked my sisters, Irene and Ivy, and took great delight in Irene's two children, Yvonne and Heather. Yvonne was about six years old at the time, and Heather about two years old.

With the ceasing of the Buzz Bombs (which were launched from Holland by the Germans) and due to the invasion of Europe by our British troops, Ernest's R.A.F. Regiment was now posted to R.A.F. Driffield in Yorkshire. That was a disappointment to both of us, for it 'put paid' to our almost weekly meetings. We both realised how fortunate we had been in those three months, to have had a chance to really get to know each other, for we discovered that our temperaments were completely opposite. Ernest was so calm, tender and kindly, and I apt to flare up when annoyed. But I knew that in really big issues I was able to act really calmly, and this streak in my character has stood me in good stead over the years.

In the lead up to Christmas 1944, the invasion was going well. Italy had capitulated and Mussolini had been disposed of, having been hung by the Italian patriots. Greece was the next to fall. Again, my brother Bill fought in Greece, and it was there that he was first wounded. He ended up fighting with the American First Army when the famous British Eighth Army had linked up with them on their final push into Berlin.

On the 8th May, 1945, the war with Germany was over. We called it V.E. Day (Victory over Europe Day). The excitement on camp knew no bounds. We all had to parade on that Wednesday morning, to be told 'officially' that war was over. We were given the rest of the day off, but of course, being in the camp post office, Marion and I had to see that all sections received their mail first.

My first thoughts were for Ernest's mother and father. The war was over; but for many of our countrymen and women it was in a way a hollow victory for they had lost sons, sweethearts, husbands and fathers. As soon as I could, I cycled over to see Ernest's mum and dad although I was due on duty that night at 6 p.m. Each person on camp, irrespective of their trade, had to do a guard duty with a sergeant and officer.

Such was my luck that my leave with Ernest was due on Saturday 11th May. Ernest's leave started on the Friday and he said he would call for me at Oakington on the Saturday. However, time was getting on and he had not arrived, so I decided to cycle over and meet him on the Willingham to Earith road. He came along smiling and saying, 'Hello Darling, the war is over.'

'Is it?' I said, feeling cross with him for being late, but with such blessed news, only momentarily. We then cycled over to Rampton to drop my things, where once again Edna and Bill Christmas put me up for the week.

At the start of our leave we thought it would be nice to celebrate it by going on the river at St. Ives, with Ernest rowing of course. It was a beautiful day, with the sun shining in a clear blue sky and everything seeming so peaceful. And Ernest and I, like so many other people, were feeling that a great weight had been lifted off our shoulders. We thoroughly enjoyed it.

We tried to tie the boat near a tree, in a secluded spot, but when we attempted to sit side-by-side in the bow, the boat tipped up and I hastily scrambled on to the bank. We enjoyed that leave, although it meant a lot of cycling for Ernest as he came over to see me each afternoon. We decided that as the war was over we did not want to continue having our leaves spoilt by the forced separation, and therefore, on our next leave, we would get married.

However, with the European war over, there was still the Japanese war to be settled. Many personnel from the R.A.F. were transferred to either the Army or Navy. Ernest being in an R.A.F. Regiment, had been transferred to the R.A.O.C. (Royal Army Ordinance Corps) in March 1945. His brother Charles was a sergeant in the R.A.O.C. Many of Ernest's pals in the R.A.F. Regiment were transferred into the Paratroop Regiment, so Ernest had a narrow escape there.

On the 15th August of that year war with Japan was ended, by the dropping of the atomic bombs, one in Hiroshima and one in Nagasaki. Naturally all the people of the country were pleased at the ending of the wars but we had no conception of the devastation that these atomic bombs caused. We did not realise what despicable weapons they were and what an atrocious substance they contained; or that in one mission they could kill millions of people and maim millions more. People are to this day suffering the horrendous effects of these terrible weapons. But at the time, we were, of course, delighted.

In the middle of June we both wrote to our people to let them know of our intentions and plans for the future. On our first thirty-six hour pass we went over to Harlesden to see May and Ralph (my sister and brother-in-law) and then to see the vicar of All Souls Church, Willesden, London NW10. This was the church where my mother and father had been married, and also my sisters, and for that reason alone I wanted to be married there. The vicar, the following week, went to see my sister May, to ascertain the true situation. Looking in the Parish Record Book they found the record of our parents' marriage and also of my sisters' and brothers' christenings. Although my family were pleased (they liked Ernest a lot) Ernest's mother said that although she was not against him marrying me, where were we going to live and what had we gathered towards our home? Seeing that everything was rationed and linen and furniture could only be got on 'Dockets' which would not be supplied until after marriage, their objection really had no substance, though I could understand her worry and that she must still be mourning the loss of Ken. But Ernest and I were just like so many other young people who were planning their futures together, now that hostilities had ceased.

The 'Dockets' that the Government were allowing, were a form of rationing. For bed linen we were able to purchase: three double sheets, four pillowcases, one bed, one mattress and three blankets. (Eiderdowns were luxuries obtained mostly on the Black Market). Ernest and I bought our furniture and most other household goods from the Peterborough Co-operative Society. We also had the opportunity to buy little extras from local sales, though at a price! Curtaining was allowed for one downstairs room and one bedroom. Plastic curtaining was available for bathrooms and kitchens, but again, it was expensive. Flooring was just enough linoleum for the main downstairs room and one bedroom. We were only allowed one table and four chairs and had to go on a waiting list to get two easy chairs and a dressing table. Factories were not geared up for producing furniture yet. The changeover from war weapons was still slowly taking place. For any extra items of furniture, one went to the market sales, and very often paid double the worth of the items procured.

Ernest was adamant that he wanted me to be married in white and my luck was in. On our camp was a young Swiss girl, Sylvain. She was visiting friends and relations in England when war was declared and that meant for her that although her country, Switzerland was neutral, the journey to return home would be too precarious and she could be interned. She decided to join the W.A.A.F. and because she was a brilliant needlewoman, she worked in the tailors' shop at R.A.F. Oakington. At the cessation of hostilities she had written to her parents stating that many of her W.A.A.F. friends were planning to get married, and her parents in their kindness, sent this lovely material for her to make a wedding dress with train. It was really exquisite. Imagine my extreme delight when one of my W.A.A.F. friends spoke to Sylvain and I was the first to wear that beautiful dress for my wedding. Both Ernest and I were overjoyed. The veil that I wore with it was a family heirloom, which had been worn by each of my sisters in turn for their weddings.

Ernest had wanted to be married in civilian clothes but because of needing coupons to buy a new suit, this became impossible for him (although he did wear 'civvies' on our honeymoon, as did I).

'What to do for a coat?' I had bought a skirt and blouse, which my sister May had managed to get for me. I also got some civilian underwear and two pairs of silk stockings. A mother and daughter, both in the W.A.A.F. at Oakington, solved the coat situation for me. One evening they came into our hut, carrying a grey blanket, which they had managed to get off the Black Market. They set about making me a coat. It was a lovely coat and I was indeed very grateful for it. It fitted me beautifully and I wore it for years. The next problem: What about shoes? My friend Joan, who had been married the

Christmas before, had a pair of thin wooden-soled shoes with brown suede tops. Problem solved! I had my going away outfit. Such was the friendship and fellow feeling of helping each other in the services.

On Thursday 15th August 1945 Ernest and I went to our respective homes to prepare for our wedding day. On Friday 17th August Ernest and his two sisters, Evelyn and Muriel, travelled up to London. They stayed at my sister May's friends' house. What joy greeted us all when we heard on the wireless that war with Japan was ended. Again a day off was given to everyone, so many of my friends from the W.A.A.F. travelled up to London to the wedding. What a wonderful thing for them to do.

Mr Edward Cooke - Uncle Ted to me - immediately agreed to give me away, when I wrote and asked him. I could not have had anyone better! He was a wonderful man and a father figure for me. I had taken Ernest to meet Uncle Ted after Ernest's return from abroad and he saw what a lovely young man he was.

ix. With fellow W.A.A.F.s at Oakington (I am middle row, far left)

x. Christmas decorations in the W.A.A.F. hut, 1943

xi. My brother Harry, in Syria, 1942

xii. Ernest and myself, at the time of our engagement

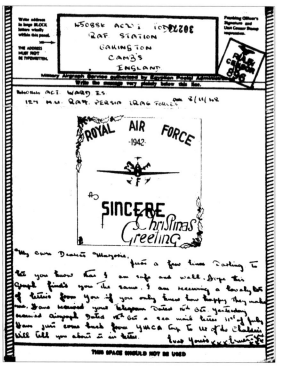

xiii. Airgram from the Middle East

xiv. Ernest with his R.A.F. pals in Palestine

xv. The young married couple, August 1945

17

We both found it hard to wait for that glorious day, the 18th August. Weather-wise, it was overcast and showery, though that did not allay our joy. Ernest's brother Dan agreed to be Best Man. His brother Charles also attended. Muriel, Ernest's younger sister was Chief Bridesmaid and Yvonne and Heather, my sister Irene's daughters, were the little bridesmaids - and lovely they were too. All three bridesmaids' dresses were borrowed from my sister May's friend. After the Reception we left at six o'clock to catch a train to Felixstowe where Dan and his wife Madeleine rented a small cottage. Dan was stationed at Felixstowe Docks whilst in the R.A.F. He and Madeleine, and their two sons, Rodney and Peter were going to Bluntisham for Dan's seven-days leave. All this was arranged so that Ernest and I could have a peaceful honeymoon in their cottage.

What a wonderful honeymoon it was. Ernest was so gentle, loving, kind and considerate, even at my disastrous attempts at cooking a meal! Being wartime, my sisters had not dared let me practise cooking at home, because of the strict rationing. Irene had bought some tinned food for us to take on honeymoon, mainly soups. Trying to show how economical I could be, I over-watered the soup first time. Ernest had gone up to bed with a heavy cold and I, wanting to show in my love for him what a caring person I was, said that I would bring up a hot bowl of soup. The soup, kidney, which I never did buy again, was like boiled water. We both sat in bed to eat it. One spoonful for me was enough. Ernest valiantly tried to consume his but noticing me put mine down on the floor, asked if I thought it was all right. I said I was just putting it down to let it cool, but no I certainly did not fancy it and neither did he. He who had gone to bed because he felt unwell with his cold, ended up going downstairs, disposing of the soup and bringing a hot cup of cocoa up for us.

The next day, Monday, we took Ernest's meat coupon to the butchers'. The butcher stated that he could only give us offal on the coupon, which was just two small pieces of liver. I had never seen liver before. 'What to do with it?' I had asked Ernest, as it was to be his birthday on the Tuesday, what he would like for a birthday present. 'You know what I would like,' he said, in such a way that I thought he was going to say something that would be far too costly for me. I said hastily, 'Now don't be stupid. I have not a lot of money.' What he went on to say was that he would like a dinner cooked by me, for a birthday treat. I felt my knees buckle!

On the Monday evening, I looked at the liver. It was terribly bloody. Ought I to clean it? I decided that I ought, so before going to bed I put it into a small mixing bowl with salt and boiling water, to let it soak overnight. It looked whitish next morning! Ernest went into the garden to pick some runner beans and dig potatoes. He had the easy job! I put on a casual dress and pinafore and tied my hair up. I was determined to look the part. 'That ought to please him,' I thought. We had bought some plums the previous day, which I did know how to cook. They only wanted stewing. But no, Ernest wanted a plum pie. 'What have I married?' I thought. Well I put the flour into the bowl. We only had two ounces of lard. 'Should I use it all?' I sliced it into pieces into the flour, then put some water with it and started stirring like mad. 'Darling,' Ernest said peering over my shoulder, 'My mother doesn't do it that way. She rubs the flour into the fat with her hands.'

I stopped stirring, turned to him and said, 'Now do not start comparing me to your mother,' but as soon as he moved away I started to rub the fat into the flour. I remembered clearly our cookery teacher at school saying, 'Now line the dish.' Well after rolling the pastry out, I did line the old-fashioned enamel dish and then put the over-stewed plums into it. Custard powder at that time was non-existent and milk was severely rationed, but there was a substitute powder called Cremola, and dried, powdered milk. Well, all dinner prepared, we sat down to eat. I was full of trepidation but Ernest was eagerly anticipating his first meal cooked by his wife of just three days. The vegetables were all right, the liver was a bit pale and a bit tough, but he knew that it was to be followed by his favourite dish of plum pie. I started to dish it up. 'Aren't you having any darling?' he asked. My reply was a big lie. 'I don't eat puddings.' As I dished the plum pie up, I not only heard but also felt the squelch. I plonked it on the plate and proceeded to camouflage it with Cremola. Enough said! I did threaten to leave him if he told his mum, but he never did. Years later, I told her, and we laughed ourselves silly. As far as I can remember, we had the rest of the meals out .

We returned to Ernest's mother's house on the Saturday, to finish our honeymoon. Our leave was extended by the extra day that was given to all forces for V.J. Day (Victory over Japan Day) and that extra day was spent at Ernest's mum's and dad's house, thank goodness. What a relief when mealtimes came! We have had many laughs over my honeymoon cooking but for me at the time, cooking that meal was a nightmare, and no doubt, for Ernest, trying to eat it must have been a nightmare too.

We returned from our leave, Ernest back to Laleham Camp near Staines, and I back to Oakington, Cambridge. I of course went to see Ernest off at Cambridge station, and indeed it was hard parting. As soon as I returned to camp, I immediately put in for my release. A quick release meant a better chance of getting a job. On the 28th September 1945, my release came through. I reported to the P.D.C. (Personnel Dispatch Centre) at R.A.F. Wythal, Birmingham, and a day later returned to my sister's home at 61 Hermitage Way, Belmont, Stanmore, Middlesex. A month later I started my job at the Air Ministry Meteorological Office at Harrow Wealdstone.

What lovely people I worked with in the Shipping Department M.O.4. The Head of M.O.4 was Commander Hennessy, and he was like a father figure to all the young people working there, very well-liked and popular. When I reported to the Air Ministry in central London, to be given my instructions as to which department I was being sent to, I met someone called Dorothy , who was also going to Harrow Weald. We became great friends, although she was put into the Administration Department. We used to meet each other at the Circle, Belmont, and travel together. One morning she saw a notice in the newsagents at the Circle, saying that there were rooms to let at Kingsbury Road, Kenton, which was only five minutes walk away from the Circle. That evening on our way home we went to enquire about the rooms and I discovered that I had met the owners of the house before, at the previous New Year's party when I was home on leave. They were Ernie and Eva Marsh, and Ernie had been my sister Ivy's driver when she worked as a conductress on the buses during the war. Well, with that, my luck was in again, and grateful indeed were Ernest and I for it.

Ernest being stationed at Laleham Camp near Staines, was able to get to Kenton each day after duty, although it meant him having to get up at 5 a.m. each morning to catch the

6 a.m. train to Waterloo, and thence to Staines. Of course there were his passes and leaves, and then exactly one year after our marriage, on the 18th August 1946, he came home demobbed! Although just three months before his demob he had been posted to Milton Road Cambridge, we counted ourselves lucky that he had been at Staines for so long. I was still working at the Air Ministry but had already decided to leave at the end of August, for our baby was due in the coming January.

Ernest went home to help with the harvest and in the September I also went to stay for a couple of weeks at his mother's house. That autumn, we decided to have a real honeymoon and went for a fortnight's holiday to Combe Martin, North Devon. We stayed at the house of a Mrs Gubb. Several of my friends at the Air Ministry had been there for their holidays and they were not remiss in their praises of the place, and of Mrs Gubb's cooking. They were right, it was beautiful cooking, and we were often supplied with a great treat - pure Devon cream!

One month after our holiday we gave up the rooms at Kenton and lived with Ernest's parents whilst waiting for our own house to be built. I had planned to have our baby at Redhill Hospital, Edgeware, Middlesex, and was attending the ante-natal clinic monthly. For these visits I travelled up to my friend Dorothy's house at Uppingham Avenue, Stanmore, and stayed overnight with her and her parents. After Christmas 1946, I was offered a home in their house until after the baby was born. Ernest and I can never thank them enough, or repay them for their kindness, which was given unstintingly. Ernest was by that time working at St. Ives, Huntingdon, and used to come up every weekend. A telegram was sent to him on Friday 31st January 1947, to say that I had gone into hospital that morning. He caught the 10 a.m. train from St. Ives to Cambridge, and from

Cambridge to Liverpool Street Station, and then on to Harrow Weald. From there he caught a bus to Belmont Circle. After having a quick cup of tea, he took a bus to Edgeware and Redhill Hospital. What should have been a comparatively short journey took him ten hours because of the appalling weather that winter, with snow lying several inches thick upon the ground.

Ernest arrived at Redhill Hospital at 8 p.m. after the end of visiting hours. They allowed him to see me for ten minutes but he did not see his baby daughter, Penelope Anne, until two days later. Great precautions were being exercised at all hospitals for there had been a countrywide epidemic of newly born babies dying of gastro-enteritis. To see his baby he had to don a sterilised gown, although he could still only look at her through a window. It was not until I took her home to Stanmore that Ernest could hold his daughter.

Such was the state of the weather that I was unable to get back to Bluntisham until the 27th February; but even then it was precarious. Ernest's friends in the village, the brothers John and Sam Hudson, volunteered to come and fetch me in their car on the 20th February, but the snow lay so thick on the ground that it was impossible for them to get through. The first opportunity presented itself on the 27th February, but even then the journey from Stanmore to Bluntisham was not easy. At Hitchin we were delayed while waiting for a snow plough to drive a pathway for us to get through. It was a great relief for Ernest and I to get to Bluntisham, and especially also a relief for Ernest's mother who had spent an anxious and worrying day. How pleased she was to hold her grand-daughter in her arms! How happy too, was Ernest's father's face! He had asked Ernest when she was born, what she looked like. Ernest had replied, 'like you about the head.' Seeing that his father was bald - he was right!

And so, for two months we were looked after by Ernest's mum. No complaint ever passed her lips at the extra washing and above all, the drying, which took place under precarious conditions, for when the snow melted, then came the floods. I remember Ernest coming back one day from Scotneys' because the factory had been flooded out. As I looked out of my mother-in-law's house from the back bedroom windows I saw drowned cattle floating down the river. It was only the embankment of the railway line that prevented the water from coming right up to the back doors of the houses along Rectory Road.

In contrast, the summer of 1947 was extremely hot. Ernest and I moved into our new house on Saturday 30th April. How my heart sang! The music of Dvorak's New World Symphony kept running through my head, the adagio of which I recalled being sung by Owen Brannigan, to the words 'Going Home.' And here I was, for the very first time in my whole life, going to my own home; with a wonderful husband and our lovely baby daughter, Penelope Anne. I had never known such joy. I was ecstatic!

18

Our home was one of the six houses that had been built in the village for ex-servicemen. A massive housing programme had been authorised throughout the country by the new Labour Government, elected in 1945 with a huge majority. The Prime Minister was Clement Atlee, who during the war had been Deputy Prime Minister to Sir Winston Churchill. In charge of the housing programme was the great Aneurin Bevan (who later on was the minister who instigated the National Health Service). What a colossal job the Housing Scheme was. The East End of London had been devastated by the Blitz of 1940-41. Then there had been the Buzz Bombs of 1944-45, sent over to devastate the country from the German installations in Holland.

What a wonderful day it was for me on the 30th April when at last I had a home of my own, or rather, when Ernest and I had a home of 'our' very own. On Sunday 1st May, after feeding Penelope, I got up and went downstairs to complete the house, by cleaning and scrubbing out the kitchen. I was in a 'Second Heaven.' The furniture was sparse but here we were, really starting our lives together. My joy knew no bounds. Happiness, Ernest and I knew, could only come by working together, using patience and understanding, and yes, we were very happy.

Ernest was still working at Tom Scotney's 'Wood Merchants,' but in July 1947 a neighbour told Ernest's brother Charles that his firm needed a lorry driver. Charles told Ernest and Ernest began working for Mr Louis Edward's 'Sand and Gravel' firm, as a driver. This at least, was better than him working at Scotney's, and the money paid was much better. I was pleased for him, or I should say 'us,' but I was also disappointed, for I always felt that he had a good brain in his head and deserved better. I had told him, when he went to the Labour Exchange in St Ives after his demob, to ask for a clerical position. But I was at Stanmore and Ernest was at Bluntisham and influenced by the people there, who said I had 'too big ideas' and who advised him to go and take whatever work was available.

Although I was delighted to have my own home at last, I found living in a small village restrictive in comparison with my previous life. People here were more reserved and were wary of newcomers. I had been used to a more communal life, with plenty of friends around me, and now I often felt lonely.

On the 27th May, 1950, our second daughter Vivienne Kathryn was born. She was a delightfully happy and engaging little girl, and an ideal companion for Penelope. On Thursday the 1st January, 1953, our first son, Alan Ernest, was born, and to complete our family, our second son, Lionel Edward, was born on Friday 10th February, 1956. Ernest and I felt how lucky we were to have such a family - and indeed we really were!

One thing that did concern and perturb me greatly, as the mother of small children, was the inadequate state of the village school. I was worried to the extent of begging Ernest to let us find somewhere else to live. The school, built in 1843 at the instigation of a Reverand Tillard, was intended mainly for the teaching of agricultural workers, or 'labourers' as they were called. The children were taught just enough 'to know their place.' The boys became landworkers, and the girls became domestic servants for the farmers and their wives. The children and their parents relied for their very existence on their employers. Without work there was no bread, and even with work, for large families, this was barely enough. Men-folk had to 'doff' their caps when meeting the farmer or his wife in the village street, and women and girls had to curtsey to show their respect to what were considered their 'betters.' This situation continued up to 1939, and coming to Bluntisham shortly after the war, I felt that I had stepped back into the Feudal System.

The school building consisted of one small side room (more like an outhouse) for the Infants, and one large room partitioned into two classrooms for the eight to eleven year olds. The eleven to fifteen year olds were all put into the Baptist Chapel schoolroom, in my view, to while away the time until they were of school leaving age. But in all fairness, I must say I was surprised by the dedication of the teachers. It must have been a tremendous job and also heart-breaking for a teacher to recognise the ability in some pupils and to know that even if they were to pass the Eleven Plus examination (that itself, to my mind a complete farce), the parents would be unable to afford to send them to the Grammar School. Such was the case in Ernest's household.

I have always set great store on education, not just as a means to a good career, but for the inevitable stimulation and the enhancement of people's lives. How extremely annoyed I was when I learned that the children at our village school had to write down their father's occupation when preparing for the Eleven Plus examination. Not until the building of St Ivo Secondary Modern School in 1957 did the so-called 'failures' have a chance to broaden their knowledge and abilities, and seek new horizons. It is an understatement to say what a tremendous relief it was to Ernest and I when we heard of the new school being built, to which children could go and be given the chance to achieve their full potential.

All four of our children attended Bluntisham village school and after that, transferred to St Ivo School. We took a keen interest in their educational development and had regular interviews with Mr Clapham the Headmaster of St Ivo School, who always treated us courteously and understood our interest in finding the right path for our children to pursue. Ernest and I were looking ahead to their adult-hood and the frustration they would feel if they were in mundane jobs, for we knew what ability they had.

Penelope our eldest did not want to stay on at school. She was always interested in hairdressing and 'out of the blue' was offered an apprenticeship by Bubbles, the proprietor of a local salon. She accepted and left school shortly before her sixteenth birthday. She became an excellent hairdresser, and in 1971 when Bubbles retired, she offered to sell the business to Penny, to 'repay her for her loyalty and hard work.' Penny accepted and when she took over, I resigned from my own job to become the receptionist, to deal with the appointments and to do the book-keeping for Penny. The business has thrived and we recently celebrated 30 years together at Maison Condor.

In 1966 our daughter Vivienne, after gaining her G.C.E 'O'levels at St Ivo School, was transferred to Ramsay Abbey Grammar School to do her 'A' levels. In 1971 our son Alan did the same. All the pupils who went from St. Ivo Secondary School to Ramsay Grammar School passed their 'A' levels extremely well. That convinced both Ernest and I what a farce the Eleven Plus was. Lionel, our youngest son, did not have to take the Eleven Plus, and he did his 'A' levels at St. Ivo School, which had by then become a comprehensive school. He also did extremely well. Vivienne, Alan and Lionel all went on to college.

All our children have done well. Today Penny continues to run her hairdressing business, Vivienne is Headteacher of a primary school, Alan is Head of Humanities at a secondary school, and Lionel has his own bookshop. Our sons and daughters-in-law have been very supportive members of the family and we have five super grandchildren: Naomi, Zoë, Imogen, Jack and Lucy.

19

Back in the early days when our children were small, Ernest and I, of course, did not know what the future would hold, but we knew that to do the best for our children meant hard work for both of us.

Ernest remained a lorry driver until 1968. In February 1961, while I was preparing dinner, a clerk from the Sand and Gravel firm came to see me to tell me that Ernest had been involved in an accident and was in hospital suffering from shock. I was taken to see him and one look at Ernest told me that it was more than shock. It later transpired that both his collarbones were broken, and all of his ribs! A doctor told me that it was a sheer miracle he had lived. I visited him each day and after a fortnight he was allowed home. The shoulder was still extremely painful. He was off work for three months and we had to fight for adequate compensation from his firm's insurance agents. Ernest was secretary of the Bluntisham, Earith and Colne Branch of the Royal British Legion and I tried to persuade him to enlist their help. After some reluctance he wrote to their Head office in London. The British Legion solicitors visited our home to speak to Ernest and although they said he had left it a little too late, they were eventually able to raise the amount of his compensation. I pointed out to Ernest, that had it been another member of the British Legion needing help, he would have lost no time in seeking it for them!

However, the accident did have one benefit in that it made Ernest more receptive to my encouragement to begin studying, with the aim of getting some qualifications and then changing his job. We both began evening classes in shorthand typing, and then later Ernest did a course in mathematics. He also studied through the School of Careers for four years. At the end of his studying, Ernest took the Civil Service Examination at Cambridge, and passed. But it meant that he would have to work in London. There was not the transport then that there is today, and I did not want to leave our home and interrupt the children's schooling when they were all doing well.

At that time I was working in the village shop, to bring in some extra money to help Penny through her apprenticeship and keep the other children on at school. A friend and customer, knew our situation, and one day her husband, Mr Hubert Parren, who was a County and District Councillor, came into the shop, bringing with him the local paper. 'Ask Ernest if he has seen this,' he said, 'and if he is interested, tell him to contact Mr Phipps.' Mr Phipps was head of the District Council employees. I went home and showed it to Ernest. He said that he had seen it, but the money was less than he was at present earning, because he was able to do overtime. I said that with my work at the shop we at least had a bit extra coming in and he should go and see Mr Phipps. Mr Parren knew about Ernest's excellent work as Clerk of the Parish Council and as secretary to the local branch of the British Legion, so he rang Mr Phipps and an interview was arranged. How pleased I was when Ernest returned to say that he had been offered the job as clerk to the engineers who were putting in main drainage to the surrounding villages of Warboys and Fenstanton, and then finally to our own village of Bluntisham. And moreover, he was going to be paid £2.00 more than he was earning already, so we would be financially better off.

Ernest was to start his duties on 1st February, 1968. The

day before that was Penelope's twenty-first birthday and her boss had given her an extra day off work, so we took her to Cambridge. We bought her a gold watch, which she had always wanted, and we had it engraved 'With love, Mum and Dad.'

The next day, Ernest started his new job. How pleased we all were for him! At last he was doing the work he was really suited for. He thoroughly enjoyed it, and liked the people he was working with, particularly his immediate boss. A few months after getting this new job, Ernest became very ill and it was discovered that he had gallstones. Once these were removed, he really was a new man and was able to enjoy his work and life in general. Our own house, being built after the war, had all modern conveniences, but many houses in the villages did not, so the main drainage programme was quite extensive. When this work eventually finished, Ernest was transferred to the Finance Office at Huntingdon, which he did not enjoy, and then finally he was moved to the Planning and Building Control Department, where he was very happy for the seventeen years until his retirement.

Having grown up in the farming village of Bluntisham, Ernest had a great love of the countryside. Growing fruit, vegetables and flowers was a natural way of life for him, and our garden was beautifully laid out and very productive. I never had to buy vegetables for the family for there was always an abundant supply whatever the season. Ernest also supplemented our income, by growing fruit on his allotment, and on a piece of land that he shared with his brothers. Particularly in the summertime he worked very long hours. In the fruit-picking season, I would pick the gooseberries and strawberries during the day and Ernest would join me after his day at work. We also helped other growers to harvest their plums, apples and pears. With the extra money we were able to pay for treats such as some memorable family holidays in Devon, and we also saved up every year to give our children a good Christmas.

When the children were small I naturally stayed at home to look after them, only working outside the home in the fruit-picking season. Then came the job at our village shop. When I left there, I worked in Ruston's shop in St. Ives for a short while. They were excellent employers and I only left when Penelope took over her hairdressing salon. We have run that business together ever since.

20

Ernest and I had a very happy and successful marriage in spite of the fact that our natures were completely opposite. But whatever interest or concern one of us had, it became a shared experience, helping each other. Our lives were very busy, but we still found time for outside interests and in particular we both had a sense of service to the community.

When our children were still at Bluntisham Primary School, Mr Holt, the head teacher called a meeting to suggest starting a Parent Teachers' Association. I attended and when nobody else volunteered, I agreed to become the secretary. When he suggested a sports day, I put forward the idea that we could make it a village sports day involving the whole community (remembering the fete days that people had enjoyed at John Groom's). We held it on a Saturday and the whole village joined in. The parish councillors readily supported us by helping to raise money to cover expenses and by giving individual donations towards it. We had 'bring and buy' and jumble sales. Everyone was very enthusiastic. Ernest acted as cashier, for the sports day prizes were monetary ones in brown pay envelopes. For the children at the village school (eleven years and under) the prizes were one shilling and sixpence - for coming first; one shilling - for coming second; and sixpence - for third place. The other children taking part all received a packet of fruit pastilles donated by the two village shopkeepers.

On the Saturday morning of each Sports Day, mothers on the committee and I went to the school and set about preparing the schoolchildren's teas. We made up little packages of sandwiches and cakes. As each child came to the playing field they were handed their packages. Adults and children not at the village school paid an entrance fee, which included a nominal price for their teas. We sold cups of tea and soft drinks from the pavilion, but again, the village school children were given theirs free.

The whole village joined in the events and had a good day. We had races for the older people, including the mums and dads. For the older boys of the village we had the mile race. They got ten shillings for winning that, seven shillings and six pence for coming second, and four shillings for third place. There was even a slow bicycle race! All this jollification went on until 8.00 to 8.30 in the evening - a heavy day's work, but a popular event enjoyed by all. When Mr Holt left the village to take over a bigger school at Cambridge, the new headmaster, after his first summer, no longer agreed with it. Many people stopped me in the street to ask why we did not continue with it. Well it was fun while it lasted!

Ernest and I soon became involved in village life in another way. When the vacancy occurred for a clerk to the parish council Ernest was approached and asked if he would accept that position. The wages were twelve pounds per annum! He was delighted to accept. Here at last was a real chance for him to be of service to Bluntisham and its people. He was a very dedicated man.

Later, I was asked to be a candidate in the forthcoming parish council election, but I failed by two votes. However at the next election, three years later, I got elected and served on the council for the next thirty years. For some of that time I became vice-chairman and then chairman of the council. In fact, when my three years as chairman of the council ended, the prospective incoming chairman asked me if I would continue for another three years. This I declined but did agree to act as vice-chairman again for him. I found my work as a councillor satisfying because I felt that I was able to influence improvements in the village. In particular I was keen to improve facilities for young people such as the provision of a new sports pavilion. As the parish council representative, I also served on the governing body of Bluntisham School and became Chair of Governors, a position that really suited me with my interest in education.

Ernest had been a Labour supporter from the age of fifteen, and he belonged to the Left Book Club. We were both socialists in our outlook and had a dedicated concern for the education and welfare of ordinary working people. We had always voted Labour, and in the late 1950s we became members of Huntingdon and District Labour Party. This involved regularly attending meetings, and helping during election campaigns.

One of our Labour Party colleagues was recruiting officer for the National Union Of Agricultural and Allied Workers and one evening he came to visit me with Ernie Hackney who was the district organiser of the N.U.A.A.W. They told me that the Bluntisham, Earith and Colne branch of the union had been suddenly let down, and that they did not now have a branch secretary. They asked me if I would take this job on, but I replied that I was not an agricultural worker and also I had very little knowledge about trade unionism. However I said that I would do it for three months to help them through this difficult period. The District Organiser took me to meet the various members and explained my duties to me, which mainly involved collecting subscriptions. I attended Union meetings in Huntingdon and was introduced to other union officials and their members. At the end of the three months I felt committed to carry on and help local members.

Although not an agricultural worker myself, of course, I had married into a family with a history of working on the land, and since coming to Bluntisham I had perceived many injustices that I thought by working for the Union, I could help to fight against. My mother-in-law had told me much about rural poverty and the social set-up before the war. She herself had experienced many hard times. She told me that she had often had to live on bread and water when food was short, except for when her husband whilst working in the fields was able to snare a rabbit; which she would make into a family meal to last for two or three days. With large families to feed, many wives had to make do with precious little. Any milk had to be given to the children because lack of milk and good food caused rickets, and there were many children suffering from this in those days. Fortunately it did not happen in Ernest's family. Husbands also had to be fed, for they were the breadwinners. I know as a fact that when my husband was young, he and his brothers and sisters would attend both Church and Chapel on Sunday, because the wealthier members of the congregation would often give them a can of milk to take home. Such was the poverty in those days. 'Crumbs from the rich man's table!' How, when I heard about it, I found myself fuming at the injustice of it all! To you, reading this now, it must seem inconceivable, but it is true. There was no welfare state then.

In many rural areas, practically the only work available was land work for the men and domestic work for the women and girls, with the girls invariably living at their place of work. Therefore, the farmer and his wife were looked upon as 'paragons of virtue' and greatly revered and feared for the power they held in the community. One hears of the slump in the '30s and it must have been as devastating in the rural areas as it was in towns and cities.

With the coming of the Second World War, things greatly improved for the farmer and farm worker. Some men in the village, in order to escape being called up into the Armed Services, though not having worked on the land before, suddenly had a great desire to do so. Of course men were needed to work on the land, although a Girls' Land Army had been formed because a land force was needed to feed the people of the nation. With the invasions by Germany, imports to England from other countries ceased. The nation was near to starving when rationing was introduced in 1940, and remained so until 1951. Beige coloured ration books were for adults and the green ones were for children. Strict rationing it was too - and if by any chance a consignment of fruit managed to get through to the country, it was totally designated to the children. If they were lucky they might possibly get a banana or an orange.

The fruit growers of Bluntisham, in an area noted particularly for the Victoria plum, now had a field day, and some became quite rich. Ernest and his brothers, although they had small pieces of land and orchards from which they earned their livings, were all called up into the Services, so their parents, already in their sixties, worked the land for them, so that they would have work and an income when they hopefully returned home. Ernest had been allowed a six months deferment but was called up into the R.A.F. in April 1941. Three of his older brothers were already in the Services; Joe and Daniel were in the R.A.F. and Charles went into the R.A.O.C. It was a year or two later that their youngest brother Ken went into the R.A.F. as a flight engineer.

At the end of the war, the social order was changing, but only slowly in the rural areas. I remember when I first came to Bluntisham from Stanmore, walking up the Bluntisham Heath road and seeing a row of men, all in a line, hoeing a piece of land. I thought what a soul destroying job that must be. There was barely any mechanisation then and the wages were miserly. No wonder their wives were still willing to supplement the family income by becoming domestic servants.

When I became secretary of the Bluntisham, Earith and Colne branch of the N.U.A.A.W. there was still a need to speak up for the betterment of conditions for agricultural workers. Wages were still grossly inadequate and the farmers were always citing that the low wages were compensated by some of the workers living rent free in farm cottages. One of my main ambitions was to see the abolition of the 'tied cottage' for it gave the farmer a hold over his workers. It not only kept wages low, but also meant that farm workers were totally subservient to their employers, through fear of eviction. Of course, men living in the cottages dare not speak out against them. As one man said 'A tied cottage ties your tongue.'

I once had to attend an eviction and I was horrified to witness the distress of the family concerned. The bailiffs came to the house very early in the morning and all the family's goods were literally thrown into the street. They had nowhere to go and as you can imagine, the poor woman was beside herself with grief and humiliation. Neighbours took some of the family's property into their houses for safekeeping.

On another occasion, a land worker come to see me late one night, having cycled eight miles in the rain because his employer had told him that if he so desired, he could evict him the very next day without giving prior notice or explanation. With my District Organiser's help we managed to get him a council house, which luckily for him, had become vacant quite quickly. He left his job, or rather, was given termination of employment, and decided to try and obtain work as a freelance gardener. Quite a few people were glad of his services and he soon got on his feet. From then on, he ignored me and I realised that people you have helped are often later embarrassed to acknowledge they know you. This did not stop me trying to help in difficult situations, but it made me wiser, and I learnt not to expect gratitude.

When I attended N.U.A.A.W. conferences I always put forward a resolution from my branch for the abolition of tied cottages. I suggested that the living accommodation should be properly evaluated and that the farm worker should have a proper rent book from the farmer. That way, a realistic wage could be paid. A farm worker, I pointed out was becoming increasingly skilful, not only in basic husbandry, but also in veterinary knowledge and in the ability to manage machinery.

In all fairness to some farmers, they too could be 'taken for a ride.' I came across one worker who used the farmer to get living accommodation for himself and his wife. After working for just two weeks on the land, he complained that his back was too painful for him to work any more. It transpired that he had indeed used the farmer just to get free shelter. As the saying goes, 'There are two sides to every coin.'

Another aspect of my job as a branch secretary, was to help members injured at work to get advice from the Trade Union Legal Department regarding their claims for compensation. I helped several people in this capacity.

In 1982 the N.U.A.A.W. was amalgamated with the Transport and General Workers Union. My name had frequently been put forward to the headquarters of the N.U.A.A.W. as a prospective delegate to the annual Labour Party Conferences, but it was not until the amalgamation with the T.G.W.U. that I was eventually elected. Needless to say I was both very surprised and also thrilled at the great opportunity. I attended several Labour Party Conferences and one year was delighted to receive an invitation to Barbara Castle's 80th birthday dinner and celebrations.

Ernest always accompanied me to the conferences, apart from one year when he was unable to come to an N.U.A.A.W. conference. That year I felt that something important was missing, in spite of all the camaraderie of fellow delegates. We made sure that this situation never occurred again and whatever either of us did in the future, it was a partnership.

At the time that Penny took over the hairdressing salon in 1972 I was already Branch secretary of the N.U.A.A.W. and Penny agreed that I could not let the Union down and should continue working for them. We also decided that our salon should be run on proper Trade Union lines. The first thing that we needed to do was to join the Hairdressers' Federation and to get a copy of the Hairdressers' Wages booklet. When we received the book we realised that the wages certainly needed updating and increasing. This we did immediately. We later had a visit from a representative of the U.S.D.A.W. and of course we allowed the staff to be interviewed by him without our presence. When he spoke to us afterwards he remarked that he wished some other salons were run like ours. There is a saying that 'the worker should be worthy of his hire,' but we believe also that 'an employer should be worthy of a good employee.' That became our criterion and has remained so.

Several of our employees have been with us for a long time and that must speak for itself. We have an excellent staff who are also our friends. Likewise, our customers are also our friends. When Penny recently celebrated thirty years as owner of Maison Condor a group of customers organised a surprise celebration for her and even went so far as to inform the local press who sent a photographer. When Ernest died, all the staff without mentioning it beforehand, turned up at the funeral. Penny and

I both found that very rewarding and comforting. I remember once going to a Hairdressers' Federation meeting with Penny, and the person conducting the meeting said that the workers were our servants! At that remark, Penny and I left the meeting and we have not attended any more, although we still subscribe to the N.H.F.

xvi. Penelope, Vivienne, Alan and Lionel, 1956

xvii. The children in 1963

xviii. Speaking at the N.U.A.A.W. Conference

ixx. At the same conference, surrounded by men. Women delegates were rare

xx. Ernest holding grand-daughter Imogen, 1985

xxi. Ernest's retirement party, August 1985

xxii. Cuddling grandson Jack, April 1995

xxiii. Ernest and I celebrate our Golden Wedding Anniversary

xxiv. Penelope and I celebrate thirty years at Maison Condor

xxv. Lionel, Vivienne, Penelope and Alan with me at Vivienne's 50th birthday party

xxvi. The five grandchildren, Boxing Day, 2002

21

In 1964 the National Industrial Relations Court was formed but the trade unions were very much against it, as the workers were not properly represented. Only the District Organiser of the union taking the worker's case to court, was allowed to attend. The situation was most unsatisfactory and these courts were eventually discarded. Instead the Industrial Relations Board was formed and each tribunal panel consisted of a lawyer and two members - one to represent the employers and the other to represent the workers or 'work people' as they were described. I was immensely surprised to receive a letter, with forms attached, asking me to fill them in and return them to the Minister of Labour (who at that time was Michael Foot). I did not think that anything would come of it for the Trade Union had previously recommended me for a Justice of the Peace and I had heard nothing from my application. However I did send the respective forms to the Ministry of Labour and was most surprised when within a week, I received a reply asking me if I would be prepared to be a member of the Industrial Tribunals Panel representing the 'work people.' Well I had to think seriously about it because there was Penny to consider.

One evening, the N.U.A.A.W. district organiser, Ernie Hackney came over to see me, to ask whether I had replied to the Ministry. I told him that I had to give it very serious thought. His reply was that they thought that I was the ideal person to represent the workers and that they would be very disappointed if I did not become a member of the panel. He added that if he were to come before a Tribunal and he saw me sitting there on the panel, he would feel that he would get a fair hearing. With that I wrote back immediately and accepted the position.

I had to attend training sessions at Cambridge and Bedford, and also to sit as an observer on a few cases. I attended my last training session on a Thursday. One of the members asked how long it was likely to be before being called to sit on a panel and he was told he would possibly have to wait a month. He also asked what would happen if the Trade Union member representing the worker did not understand the law. The reply was that if he thought that trade union members did not understand the law he was in for a shock, for 'they understand the law perfectly.' To say the least, I felt very pleased at that reply!

I returned to the salon and told Penny that it would be about a month before I would be called to sit on a tribunal. The next day I was at Penny's house because she was having some carpeting put down and she had asked me to stay there until it was done. At about three o'clock in the afternoon I received a telephone call from the Cambridge Tribunal Office asking me if I could be available to do a three-day case on the following Tuesday, Wednesday and Thursday. I agreed to do it, and of course informed Penny, who had put the telephone call through from the salon to her house.

It was with some nervousness that I went the following Tuesday to the Tribunal office at Sussex Street, Cambridge. Before commencing the case, the chairman of the panel would have a chat with us to discuss it. In those days you received the papers a few day before the panel met, in order to familiarise yourself with the case and make notes. To my consternation, the chairman remarked that this case would go down in history as the last one to be dealt with by the N.I.R.C. and that they would rely on my knowledge of trade unions to guide them. The case was indeed rare for I perceived, as did the chairman and the other member of the panel representing the employers, that both the County Council for whom he worked and the trade union to which he belonged, would be pleased to be rid of this man - he was a thorn in the flesh! One could sympathise with both the employers and the trade union concerned. At the end of the case a compromise was reached and the employers found a different job for the man. He was not satisfied with this and made several unnecessary demands. What became of him I never knew, but I was greatly impressed and amazed at the courteousness and patience that his employers and also the chairman of the tribunal, extended to him.

After three years as a tribunal member you would receive an official letter thanking you for your services. If they wanted you to continue as a member, another letter would be sent asking if you would be prepared to serve another three years. I served as a tribunal member for sixteen years. I enjoyed the work very much and met on equal terms many interesting people. One chairman that I worked with impressed me very much. He was a real gentleman. His name was James Freeman and he was popular with all the panel members. I later discovered that he was the brother of John Freeman, our Ambassador to America for the Labour Government in the Sixties. John was also at one time, editor of the New Statesman. James Freeman was a lawyer and he later became Head of all the tribunal members. He was a very fair and astute man, and an honour to know. Sadly, he died at a comparatively young age.

One had to retire at seventy, and my last three years finished when I was sixty-nine. I feel that a lot of my success as a member of the Industrial Tribunal Board can be put down to my excellent upbringing at John Groom's Orphanage, for while there we met many famous people and were allowed to chat to them in a normal way. I feel that subconsciously we were learning how to properly conduct ourselves in conversation and behaviour with 'all people.' I am truly very thankful for having been brought up at such a good place as John Groom's in the 1920s and 1930s.

22

When the children were small, apart from occasional day trips to the seaside, we could not afford a proper holiday. However, one year (1965 when Lionel our youngest child was nine) I saw an advertisement in the local paper, for a holiday cottage in Appledore, North Devon. I wrote and booked the cottage and we hired a car for that week. We took the children to all the places that we had visited ourselves years before, on our delayed honeymoon in Combe Martin. We enjoyed it so much that we booked the same cottage for the following year, but in the meantime we had managed to buy our own car. Ernest loved driving and was thrilled to at last have a car of his own.

After the children had grown up Ernest and I had some wonderful holidays together, travelling all over England, Scotland and Wales. Scotland became our favourite holiday venture for the scenery was so beautiful, the mountains were so magnificent, and the hospitality was second to none. We also appreciated the mountain area of North Wales. England of course, has its Lake District and in North Devon there is beautiful scenery such as the Valley of the Rocks in Lynton and Lynmouth. We also had a beautiful holiday in the Peak District of Derbyshire and the dales such as Dovedale and Monsul Dale. Yes, we found much pleasure in the everyday scenes in the life of our own beloved country. We did go abroad once, to Austria, but for us, we realised, it was a big mistake. We were averse ever after that, to organised holidays.

The best holiday accommodation that we ever experienced

was at the T.G.W.U. hotel at Eastbourne. All rooms were en-suite, the food and entertainment were excellent, and above all the staff and other guests were all very helpful and friendly. We had first stayed at this hotel when I was a delegate at a T.G.W.U. conference. When not being used as a conference centre however, the hotel was available for holiday booking by T.G.W.U. members, and Ernest and I stayed here several times. We also stayed at the T.G.W.U. hotel at Scarborough.

Once the children had grown up and married, Ernest and I found that our relationship was as strong as it had ever been. We still enjoyed each other's company and always had lots of shared interests to discuss. We had some good friends in the area with whom we shared many happy social occasions. The family remained close and there were regular visits to see children and grandchildren. On the 18th August 1985 the family organised a surprise Ruby Wedding Anniversary party for us, and ten years later, Ernest and I celebrated our Golden wedding Anniversary with a party at Alan's house.

Ernest retired from work at the Huntingdon District Council offices, in the Building Control and Planning department, at the age of sixty-five years, in 1985. He did not want to retire and I feel that in this day and age, retirement should be a gradual progression, starting with part retirement. People live for much longer today and often do not feel ready, to put it bluntly, 'for the scrap heap.' I feel also that many businesses would benefit from their expertise that could be passed on to the younger generation. With a little forethought I am sure that a plan could be worked out for them - and not to do so is to the country's loss.

Retirement did mean that Ernest was able to give more time and service to the village. He was Clerk to the Parish Council for twenty-eight years and Services Secretary for the Royal

British Legion for forty-two years, covering the villages of Bluntisham, Earith and Colne. For this work he received the highest honour, which was the British Legion Gold Badge. Many people came to our door to seek his help, which being the caring man he was, he gave unstintingly. One thing that relieved me in his retirement was the fact that he did not have to get up at five in the morning to get the Parish Council report and agenda typed out for distribution to councillors before each forthcoming meeting.

In the early days of his retirement, while I was still working at Penny's salon, Ernest began drafting his first book entitled 'Bluntisham, A Village Remembered.' It was published in 1989 and a second book entitled 'War-Time Experiences And Changes In Village Life After The War,' soon followed.

Unfortunately, Ernest's health began to deteriorate in the early 1990s. One contributory factor was the shock he felt when in 1991 his elder brother Dan died suddenly. Dan's death caused him a lot of distress and anguish and it was at about this time that we gradually began to notice that something was seriously wrong. I must record here that not once did I ever hear Ernest complain. He had had several serious illnesses throughout his life and had always borne them stoically. He was a very courageous man and until his death in 1998 he remained gentle and uncomplaining. When one hears talk of a 'Christian man' my thoughts immediately fly to Ernest, for that indeed is what he was. He had attended Bluntisham Baptist Chapel from boyhood, and in spite of his dementia, he always knew where his Chapel was. Each Sunday morning he would attend the service. In that chapel he found a true and kindly friend in the previously retired Baptist Minister, the Reverend Wilfred Chapman, who always made a point of shaking his hand and speaking to him. This was an act of kindness and friendliness that Ernest looked forward to every Sunday.

After the Sunday morning service, the congregation adjourns to the chapel's Sunday school room for a biscuit and cup of tea. Ernest always enjoyed this, for although he was shy, he truly loved the company of people. One Sunday after chapel, he did not arrive home for his dinner. I kept going to look for him and was almost frantic with worry by the time he eventually arrived home at 2.30 p.m. I asked him where he had been. 'Walking,' he said, but when I asked him where, he did not know. From then on, as he knew his way to the chapel, I would watch Ernest go up 'The Walk' (a closed path with hedges either side), and then at 12.30p.m. I would go and meet him to see him safely back

Ernest lived his life as he professed to believe. His stoicism was unshakeable. He was a wonderful, gentle and trustworthy man, who did not deserve the dreadful dementia inflicted upon him. Over and over again I thank God for having been married to Ernest. He was 'THE BEST'. He died on the 6th September, 1998. It is very hard for me, writing at the end of this autobiography, for I am incessantly reminded of the great loss that I have sustained.

'My Best Friend,' was his favourite song. One day I was muttering and grumbling over some trivial incident and he called me in from the kitchen to the dining room where he was just finishing his breakfast with the radio on.

'Darling, listen to this song,' he said. It was Don Williams singing My Best Friend. 'That's what you are to me.'

I replied that he was only saying that to make me feel guilty for grumbling and he gave his usual chuckle. But I was so pleased and happy that when I went to St. Ives that morning, I went straight to the record shop and bought that disc. This became 'our song' and until Ernest died I played the tape to him every night before we settled down to sleep. I still play it now, each night before I settle down alone, to seek comfort before I sleep; but the remembrance brings many tears.

I still have all the letters that Ernest wrote to me, throughout his time abroad and in the early days of our marriage when he was still in the Forces and we were living apart. There are several hundred of these letters, dated from 1942 to 1946, and a few from 1947 when I was at Stanmore before Penny was born. I re-read these letters frequently although I need no reminding of what a wonderful husband he was.

Yes, Ernest was a loving husband and my best friend. He is irreplaceable, and always will be. His stature in my life and in that of our whole family is greater than ever before, and always will be. My philosophy in life has been 'If one door closes, another one opens,' but the door has not closed on Ernest's and my life for he lives on 'Always In My Heart' and the hearts of our wonderful family.

As Vivienne's husband Peter would say (and as all our family would agree),

'ABSOLUTELY.'